Medieval Academy Reprints for Teaching 19

Medieval Academy Reprints for Teaching

First published in 1972
This edition is reprinted by arrangement with
The Society for Promoting Christian Knowledge.

Canadian Cataloguing in Publication Data

Morris, Colin, 1928–
    The discovery of the individual, 1050–1200

(Medieval Academy reprints for teaching; 19)
First published in 1972.
Includes bibliographical references and index.
ISBN 0-8020-6665-8

1. Individualism – History.   2. Civilization,
Medieval – 12th century.   3. Civilization, Medieval.
I. Medieval Academy of America.   II. Title.
III. Series.

B824.M65 1987   1419.4909021   C87-008463-1

Colin Morris

THE DISCOVERY OF
THE INDIVIDUAL, 1050–1200

Published by University of Toronto Press
Toronto   Buffalo   London
in association with the Medieval Academy of America

Contents

Foreword by V. H. H. Green, D.D.   xi

Preface   xiii

Chronological Table   xv

1 THE QUESTION   1
   The Individual in Western Tradition   1
   Origins   10

2 THE BACKGROUND, 900–1050   20

3 NEW LEARNING IN A NEW SOCIETY   37
   A Society in Transformation   37
   The French Renaissance   48
   The Return to the Past   51
   The Problem of Authority   57

4 THE SEARCH FOR THE SELF   64
   "Know Yourself"   65
   Confession   70
   The New Psychology   76
   Autobiography   79
   The Portrait   86

5 THE SELF AND OTHER SELVES   96
   Friendship   97
   Love: the Troubadours   107

6 THE INDIVIDUAL AND SOCIETY   121
   Satire   122
   Chrétien de Troyes   133

7 THE INDIVIDUAL AND HIS RELIGION   139
     The Passion   139
     Eschatology   144
     Mystical Theology   152

8 CONCLUSION   158

   References   169

   Suggestions for Further Reading   179

   Index   183

List of Illustrations

Facing p.

1 Tomb-slab of Rudolf of Suabia (d. 1080). Merseburg Cathedral 126
   (*Bildarchiv Foto-Marburg*)

2 Enamel plaque of Count Geoffrey of Anjou (d. 1151). Museum
   at Le Mans 126
   (*Archives Photographiques, Paris*)

3 Head of Frederick Barbarossa. Made 1155/71. Cappenberg 127
   (*The Author*)

4 Tombs of Henry II (d. 1189) and Eleanor of Aquitaine (d.
   1204). Abbey church of Fontevrault 127
   (*Archives Photographiques, Paris*)

5 Crucifixion from façade of abbey of Saint-Mesme. Museum
   at Chinon. Tenth century 142
   (*Archive Société des Amis du Vieux Chinon*)

6 Gero Cross. Cologne Cathedral. Late tenth century 142
   (*Bildarchiv Foto-Marburg*)

7 Crucifixion scene from Codex Egberti. Late tenth century.
   Trier 143
   (*Bildarchiv Foto-Marburg*)

8 Crucifixion, Three Kings Casket. About 1200. Cologne 143
   (*Bildarchiv Foto-Marburg*)

Acknowledgements

Thanks are due to the following for permission to quote from copyright sources:

The Bodleian Library, Oxford: lines quoted from Lawrence of Durham

Burns & Oates Ltd: *The Letters of Saint Bernard of Clairvaux*, by B. S. James

The Clarendon Press: *Oxford Book of Medieval Latin Verse*, ed. F. J. E. Raby

Constable & Co. Ltd: *Medieval Latin Lyrics*, tr. Helen Waddell

J. M. Dent & Sons Ltd and E. P. Dutton & Co. Inc.: *Arthurian Romances of Chrétien de Troyes*, tr. W. W. Comfort (Everyman Library Edition)

Faber & Faber Ltd and Random House Inc.: *About the House*, by W. H. Auden

Harvard University Press: *Letters of Peter the Venerable*, ed. Giles Constable

Dr R. D. Laing: the title of chapter 4, suggested by his book, *The Self and Others* (Tavistock Publications)

The Macmillan Company, New York: the title of chapter 6, suggested by *The Individual and his Religion*, by G. W. Allport

Methuen & Co. Ltd: *English Historical Documents*, Vol. II, by D. C. Douglas and G. W. Greenaway

Oxford University Press: *English Hymnal*, 95, tr. Percy Dearmer

Phaidon Press Ltd: *Life in Medieval France*, by J. Evans

Routledge & Kegan Paul Ltd: *The Autobiography of Guibert, Abbot of Nogent*, tr. C. C. S. Bland

University of Notre Dame Press: *The Lineage of Lady Meed*, by J. A. Yunck

Foreword

In this book Professor Morris presents a scholarly reappraisal of the origins of a concept which we have come to take for granted as an essential attribute of Western Christian society, that of the individual. He traces this back to the rich, mobile civilization of medieval Europe in the twelfth century. It is perhaps surprising that, in spite of the many specialized works which have contributed to our understanding of medieval civilization, so many misconceptions persist about its character. A politician who wishes to use a pejorative adjective is likely to select the word "medieval". For the schoolboy the modern world still starts with the Renaissance in which he finds much which he supposes antithetical to medieval society; in the teaching of the fifteenth-century humanists he discovers first the concept of individualism which he believes to be an essential characteristic of the post-sixteenth-century world. In fact, many of the features which we associate with the Renaissance appeared in the medieval world.

When the concept of individuality first developed remains a controversial question; but Professor Morris, drawing on literary, historical, and theological, as well as artistic, sources, attributes the discovery of the individual to the spiritually and intellectually dynamic world of the twelfth century. It was a society which was in some respects confronted with problems not wholly dissimilar from those of the twentieth century. His argument, fascinating and convincing, will surely prove of interest not merely to historians, linguists, and theologians, but to all those who are concerned with the life-line which binds the modern Church to the medieval world.

V. H. H. GREEN

Preface

The distinction between the "medieval" and the "modern" world is a fixed part of the historian's terminology, but it probably obscures the truth rather than clarifies it. Many "modern" attitudes and institutions may be traced back to the great cultural changes which took place in western Europe in the decades around 1100. This book is an attempt to examine one of these, and to consider what signs may be discovered at that time of the respect for, and interest in, the individual, which was to be so marked a feature of later Western culture. It is certainly not designed as a total picture of twelfth-century ways of thought, but, while sticking closely to the theme of interest in the individual, I have deliberately sought examples across the frontiers which are often drawn between history, literature, theology, and the visual arts.

Some of the writers considered here have received relatively little discussion, at least in English, but a few have been the centre of a secondary literature of embarrassing abundance. To have discussed, as fully as they deserve, the various interpretations of the troubadour ideal of love would have distorted the balance of the book hopelessly, for the troubadours are no more important to the central theme than are the Latin satirists, about whom much less has been written. In certain instances, therefore, it has been necessary (like the pamphleteer of old) to take a brief way with dissent, although I have attempted always to indicate when an opinion is a matter of controversy.

It is part of the purpose of the book to introduce readers to twelfth-century literature by including a substantial number of quotations. In the case of poetry, it seemed faint-hearted to provide a prose rendering which contained none of the spirit of the original, and I have therefore tried my hand at a translation into an appropriate English verse-form. There is an admitted danger here of distorting a poet's true meaning because of the requirements of English rhyme or, worse still, of the author's argument, and I have often included the original text, so that the reader can keep his eyes open for foul play.

The writer of a general study is bound to be heavily in the debt of others, and the suggestions for further reading and the footnotes indicate some of the scholars to whom I have been particularly indebted. To the names mentioned there, I would like to add those of Miss Beryl Smalley and Dr W. A. Pantin, to whose scholarship and personal friendship I owe a great deal. In addition I have received generous personal help. My thanks are especially due to Mrs D. R. Sutherland, who kindly advised me about the study of troubadour poetry, and whose comments saved me from many mistakes and ill-founded views; and to Dr R. W. Southern, President of St John's College, Oxford, who read the draft of the whole book in typescript, and whose views were of the greatest value, both in the clarification of the line of argument and the correction of particular errors. I am also indebted, for comments and advice on specific points, to a number of friends and colleagues, among them Dr J. M. Wallace Hadrill, Mr Hugh Farmer, Mr Douglas Gray, the Reverend H. E. J. Cowdrey, and M. l'abbé J. Pohu, of Fontevrault; and I have benefited from the discussion of particular themes in this book with groups at the University of Reading and the Theological Colleges of Wells and Cuddesdon. I would also like to acknowledge the help of my cousin, Mrs Margaret Holmes, who patiently typed a great part of the book, and of the Master and Fellows of Pembroke College, Oxford, who made its writing possible by giving me a period of leave from normal academic duties.

For the opinions, and the mistakes, I am of course solely responsible.

Southampton 1972   COLIN MORRIS

Chronological Table

The table below sets out in chronological order some works and writers mentioned in the text, and fixes them in relation to a few other events of importance. Only rarely can a book be dated to an exact year, and the table should be regarded as only approximate. Where the margin of error exceeds two or three years, a span of years, or a question mark, is shown.

1050?	*Ruodlieb*
1053?	Birth of Guibert of Nogent
1056	Death of Emperor Henry III
1066	Norman conquest of England
1070	Death of Otloh of Saint Emmeram
1072	Death of Peter Damiani
1073	Gregory VII elected Pope
1078	Death of John of Fécamp
1080	Deposition of Henry IV proclaimed Tomb monument of Rudolf of Suabia
1080?	*Song of Roland* in substantially its present form
1086	Succession of William IX to Aquitaine and Poitou
1090	Ivo appointed Bishop of Chartres
1093	Saint Anselm appointed Archbishop of Canterbury
1095	First Crusade preached at Clermont
1096	Hildebert of Lavardin appointed Bishop of Le Mans
1098	Foundation of Cîteaux Anselm, *Cur Deus Homo*
1099	Jerusalem captured by First Crusade

1100   Succession of Henry I in England

1104   Guibert appointed Abbot of Nogent

1108   Guibert, *Gesta Dei per Francos*
         Succession of Louis VI in France

1109   Death of Anselm of Canterbury

1114   Abelard teaching in Paris

1115   Bernard appointed Abbot of Clairvaux

1116   Guibert's autobiography completed

1117   Death of Anselm of Laon

1120   William of Saint Thierry, *The Nature and Dignity of Love*

1122   Concordat of Worms

1123   Abelard, *Sic et Non*
         Death of Guibert of Nogent

1127   Death of William IX

1128/40 Abelard, *Paraclete Hymnbook*

1129/41 Bernard, *de diligendo Deo*

1130/40 William of Saint Thierry, *The Nature of Body and Soul*

1133   Abelard, *Commentary on Romans* and *Historia Calamitatum*
         Death of Hildebert

1134   Aelred became monk at Rievaulx
         New west front begun at Chartres

1135   Abelard, *Ethics*
         William of Saint Thierry became Cistercian at Signy

1135–53 Bernard at work on his sermons on Song of Songs

1135–60 Hugh 'Primas' of Orleans writing

1137   Succession of Louis VII in France
         His marriage with Eleanor of Aquitaine
         Lawrence of Durham, *Hypognosticon*
         Marcabru at work

1140   Abelard condemned by Council of Sens, at instance of Saint Bernard and William of Saint Thierry

1140?   Bernard of Cluny, *Hora novissima*

1142   Death of Abelard

1143   Aelred, *The Mirror of Charity*

1144   Consecration of east end of Saint-Denis, newly built by Abbot Suger

1145?   Early work of Bernard of Ventadour

1145   Otto of Freising, *The Two Cities*

1147   Aelred appointed Abbot of Rievaulx

1148   Death of William of Saint Thierry

1148?   Death of Jaufre Rudel

1150   Peter Lombard, *Sentences*
          Bernard of Clairvaux, *de consideratione*

1150?   "Self-portrait" of Eadwine of Canterbury

1151   Memorial tablet of Geoffrey of Anjou

1152   Marriage of Henry of Anjou and Eleanor of Aquitaine
          Frederick Barbarossa elected King of Germany

1153   Death of Bernard of Clairvaux

1154   Henry of Anjou King of England

1155?   Bernard of Ventadour in England at court of Henry II

1155   Imperial coronation of Frederick Barbarossa

1155/71   Making of Cappenberg head

1159   John of Salisbury, *Metalogicon* and *Policraticus*
          Election of Alexander III as Pope

1164   Archpoet, *Confession*

1165   Aelred *de Anima* and *de Spirituali Amicitia* completed

1166   Walter of Châtillon in service of Henry II

1167   Death of Aelred

1170   Murder of Thomas Becket

1170?   Chrétien de Troyes, *Erec and Enide*

1180   Death of John of Salisbury

1180?   Chrétien, *Knight of the Lion* and *Knight of the Cart*

1185?   Chrétien, *The Story of the Grail*

1187   Fall of Jerusalem to Saladin

1189   Death of Henry II of England

1190?   Death of Walter of Châtillon

1200?   Nicholas of Verdun, casket of Three Kings at Cologne

1200?   Tomb of Henry II at Fontevrault

1 *The Question*

THE INDIVIDUAL IN WESTERN TRADITION

Some thirty inches from my nose
The frontier of my Person goes;
And all the untilled air between
Is private *pagus* or demesne.
Stranger, unless with bedroom eyes
I beckon you to fraternize,
Beware of rudely crossing it;
I have no gun, but I can spit.[1]

Auden's words describe an experience of individual identity which is familiar to most of us. We think of ourselves as people with frontiers, our personalities divided from each other as our bodies visibly are. Whatever ties of love or loyalty may bind us to other people, we are aware that there is an inner being of our own; that we are individuals. To the Western reader it may come as a surprise that there is anything unusual in this experience. It is to us a matter of common sense that we stand apart from the natural order in which we are set, subjects over against its objectivity, and that we have our own distinct personality, beliefs, and attitude to life. In part, of course, we are justified in thinking that this is a common element in human psychology. Every adult human being is aware of a distinction between himself and the people and things around him. Nevertheless, it is true that Western culture, and the Western type of education, has developed this sense of individuality to an extent exceptional among the civilizations of the world. In primitive societies the training of the child is usually directed to his learning the traditions of the tribe, so that he may find his identity, not in anything peculiar to himself, but in the common mind of his people. Consider, for example, this advice given to his

son by a West African father, and contrast it with the words of
Auden quoted above:

> There is a certain form of behaviour to observe, and certain
> ways of acting in order that the guiding spirit of our race may
> approach you also. . . . If you desire the guiding spirit of our race
> to visit you one day, if you desire to inherit it in your turn, you
> will have to conduct yourself in the selfsame manner; from now
> on, it will be necessary for you to be more and more in my
> company.[2]

This relative weakness of the sense of individuality is not confined
to those societies which we normally call primitive. The student of
the Greek Fathers or of Hellenistic philosophy is likely to be made
painfully aware of the difference between their starting-point and
ours. Our difficulty in understanding them is largely due to the
fact that they had no equivalent to our concept "person", while
their vocabulary was rich in words which express community
of being, such as οὐσια, which in our usage can be translated
only by the almost meaningless word "substance". The Asiatic
and Eastern tradition of thought has set much less store by the
individual than the West has done. Belief in reincarnation virtually
excludes individuality in the Western sense, for each person is but
a manifestation of the life within him, which will be reborn, after
his apparent death, in another form. Western individualism is
therefore far from expressing the common experience of humanity.
Taking a world view, one might almost regard it as an eccentricity
among cultures.

Yet it is an eccentricity of great historical importance, because
of the dominant role played by the West during the past five centuries, during which European power and European values have
deeply influenced the development of other continents. Individualism takes many forms, and before we investigate its origins in our
own culture, it will be necessary to outline the sense in which we
shall understand it. With one of its more obvious manifestations
this book will not be much concerned. Political thought in the
West has been deeply influenced by individualistic assumptions.
Whereas Aristotle began from the *polis*, the city which to him was
the natural unit of society, the "classical" Western political

philosophers (among whom one must count Hobbes, Locke, and Rousseau) assumed that the individual person and his rights pre-existed any form of society. No modern writer, perhaps, would now adopt so extreme an assumption, but the idea that the individual has certain rights which society cannot properly take from him, is far from dead. It is embodied in the constitution of some modern states (notably that of the U.S.A.) and it lies behind many contemporary declarations about Human Rights.

This book will not be concerned with the origins of this political individualism, but with individualism at a more directly personal level: with that respect for individual human beings, their character and opinion, which has been instilled into us by our cultural tradition, and with its implications for personal relationships and beliefs. The hard core of this individualism lies in the psychological experience with which we began: the sense of a clear distinction between my being, and that of other people. The significance of this experience is greatly increased by our belief in the *value* of human beings in themselves. Humanism may not be the same thing as individualism (we shall have to consider this point later), but they are at least first cousins, for a respect for the dignity of man is naturally accompanied by a respect for individual men. On the reality of this respect for man's capacities, it is perhaps fair to use Shakespeare as evidence:

> What a piece of work is a man! How noble in reason! how infinite in faculty! in form, in moving, how express and admirable! in action, how like an angel! in apprehension, how like a god! the beauty of the world! the paragon of animals![3]

In Christian tradition, this confidence in the individual's value has been expressed in the belief in his continued life after death. The implications of this were vividly stated by C. S. Lewis: "There are no *ordinary* people. You have never talked to a mere mortal. Nations, cultures, arts, civilizations—these are mortal, and their life is to ours as the life of a gnat."[4] In ethics there has been a similar tendency to assert the supreme value of the individual. This conviction lies behind Kant's famous dictum that a man must be treated as an end, and never as a means, and it has recently been argued to be the corner-stone of European ethics: "The idea of the individual person as of supreme worth is fundamental to the moral, political and religious ideals of our society."[5]

It is therefore natural to find that Western literature has shown a strong interest in personal character. Europe has developed literary forms specially devoted to the exploration of the individual and his relationships, such as biography, autobiography, and the novel; forms which are unknown, or relatively undeveloped, in other cultures. There is also much truth in the view that the Greek tragedy was a drama of circumstance, whereas the Western tragedy is essentially a drama of character. The personal character of Oedipus is really irrelevant to his misfortunes, which were decreed by fate irrespective of his own desires. Conversely, the tragedies of Shakespeare turn on the flaw in the hero's own character. Othello would have had no difficulty in dealing with Hamlet's problem, nor Hamlet with Othello's. Even where there is a prophecy of doom spoken at the beginning of the play, as in *Macbeth*, we still feel that Macbeth and Lady Macbeth are the authors of their own destruction. "The fault, dear Brutus, is not in our stars, but in ourselves, that we are underlings."[6] The same concern with individuality may be found in painting, in which the portrait has played an important part. In a good portrait, we hope to find both the physical representation of a man's appearance and a reading of his character. Nor has the fascination with human character been confined to the observation of other men. There has also been in Western literature a strong element of self-discovery, expressed in highly personal lyric poetry or in the stress of personal experience in religion. This "inwardness" or acute self-awareness has been a distinctive feature of Western man.

These have been the main characteristics of Western individualism, as it will concern us in this book. It has not been equally influential throughout the whole period from 1500 to 1900; it has always met with some criticism or counter-action, and in some periods individualism has subsided almost completely under the weight of authority or convention. Yet it has been a very prominent feature of Western civilization during centuries in which the West has profoundly influenced the development of the rest of the world. It may be added that it now appears doubtful whether the old individualism will long survive; whether, indeed, some of its main features have not already disappeared. That is not the subject of this study, but it perhaps increases still further the interest of an inquiry into the historical circumstances which brought about the discovery of the individual in the West.

The conventional account of the discovery of the individual attributes it to the Italian Renaissance of the fifteenth century. Until that time, it is often supposed, a powerful hierarchy had enforced rigorously orthodox modes of thinking upon the peoples of the West, until a new freedom was achieved by the rediscovery of classical humanism. Accompanied as this was by a return to the reading of the Fathers of the Church, and by the recovery of the of the Greek New Testament, it had an explosive effect upon thought and art. Self-expression, a respect for human reason, and a delight in the varieties of individuals arose to challenge, if not entirely to replace, the uniformity dictated by authority. Thinking of this sort helps to account for the conventional distinction between "medieval" and "modern" history, the dividing-line of which has been placed about 1500. This analysis of the situation is still prevalent, not only in old-fashioned text-books, but in studies of scholarly importance. For instance, Bishop Stephen Neill has written that:

> The Middle Ages were dominated by theology; and it is not surprising that the imaginative approach to the problems of human personality is rare until the Middle Ages begin to pass over into the Renaissance.[7]

That the achievements of the Italian Renaissance were great, no one would deny. An Erasmus or a Michaelangelo were able to express the human spirit in a way which would have been impossible fifty years before. Yet the more carefully the Renaissance is studied, the more evident it becomes that it was deeply rooted in the work of the preceding centuries. Luther's thought would have been inconceivable without the theology of the late medieval schoolmen; the cultivation of Latin letters goes well back into the history of the Italian universities; and the new forms of the visual arts can be traced back to Cimabue and Giotto about the year 1300. The very idea of the "Renaissance" itself was a late medieval one, rooted in the expectations of a Golden Age entertained by

prophets and preachers long before 1500.[8] The idea of a sudden
rebirth of humanism in the late fifteenth century rested, moreover,
on a very simple-minded view of the Middle Ages. In practice it
was certainly not a pure "age of faith", free from the challenge
of a secular view of man and uncomplicated by the use of human
reason. For these reasons, Walter Ullmann, in his important book
The Individual in Medieval Society, traces the origin of the new
modes of thinking to a period far earlier than the fifteenth century.
He sees some hints of them in the twelfth century, and growing
development towards the formulation of an idea of the individual
during the thirteenth and fourteenth centuries. He has thus
radically revised the older view of the Renaissance. The general
pattern of the graph, so to speak, is still the same, for it shows a
continuous progress towards a true concept of individuality.
Instead of a rapid rise beginning about 1450, we have a steady
ascent beginning as far back as 1200. There can be no doubt that,
by taking adequate account of recent study of late medieval
society, Professor Ullmann has produced a picture much closer
to the truth. It must be appreciated, however, that the subject
of his book is the individual's status in society, and particularly
the emergence of the idea of a citizen, possessed of his own rights
and equal before the law. He is dealing, in other words, with that
political individualism which will not be a major theme in this
book. It is important to bear this in mind, for we have now to
consider an entirely different interpretation of the discovery of
the individual. The divergence between the two accounts arises
as much from differing subject-matter as from a disagreement over
interpretation.

The alternative reading* of the course of events is perhaps most
fully examined in R. R. Bolgar's work *The Classical Heritage and
its Beneficiaries*, but has also been powerfully stated by Dom
David Knowles.[9] These writers see the twelfth century as a distinctively humanistic age; a point of view often associated with
the title, the twelfth-century Renaissance. One aspect of the

* For another important analysis of twelfth-century humanism,
which differs substantially from those mentioned in the text, see R. W.
Southern, "Medieval Humanism", *Medieval Humanism and Other
Studies* (Oxford 1970) pp. 29–60.

enormously increased vitality of the age was a new respect for man and human possibilities. This humanism, however, was in the end frustrated, for a series of reasons which we must consider later. The graph sketched here is obviously very different from the one which we have so far been considering. There is a rapid rise in individualism and humanism in the years from about 1080 to 1150. Then, however, a peak was reached, which was followed by a progressive decline. Then, once more, the graph turned upwards, eventually to reach the new heights of the Italian Renaissance, which by the late fifteenth century had transcended all previous humanistic achievement. To talk in such terms is, of course, to oversimplify. One's reading of the course of events will depend on the criteria which are employed. If our main interest is in the role of the individual citizen within the political community, we shall certainly not find that this was a major achievement of the twelfth century. If we concentrate more on the development of self-awareness and self-expression, on the freedom of a man to declare himself without paying excessive attention to the demands of convention or the dictates of authority, then we may well find that the twelfth century was in this respect a peculiarly creative age. It is in this sense that Bolgar discerns in it "for the first time the lineaments of modern man".[10]

So far I have written somewhat ambiguously, as if "individualism" and "humanism" are the same thing. They are unquestionably connected, but it is important for us to consider more closely the relationship between the two. An examination of humanism as a concept is no mere matter of correct definition; it raises many of the most important questions which will confront us in a study of the period between 1050 and 1200. As applied to the twelfth, or for that matter to the sixteenth, century, the word carries two connotations. At a technical level it implies the ability to read Latin easily and to write it elegantly. (At Oxford, the course in classics still rejoices in the title Literae Humaniores, Humane Letters.) It may appear at first sight that skilful Latinity is a technical accomplishment which has little connection with individualism or any other view of life, but for the men of the age it was an essential preliminary to the imaginative exploration of themselves and the universe. What cannot be verbalized can scarcely be thought, and before 1050 the capacity of most writers to express themselves lucidly was poor. When, in the ninth century, Einhard attempted to describe Charlemagne's personal appearance—a bold undertaking, for there were few recent precedents to guide him—he built up a pastiche of quotations from Suetonius, to such an extent that some commentators have suspected that the passage is not a description of Charlemagne from the life, but a merely literary construction. It must be added that awkward writing of this sort did not stop with the coming of the twelfth century. The curse of medieval literature in general was a readiness to be content with descriptions which were dictated purely by convention or were copied from another, sometimes an inappropriate, source.[11] If we seek for genuinely individual description from the life, we must look to men who were able to write down fluently and naturally what they saw, men such as Guibert of Nogent or Peter of Blois. The same is true of the art of self-expression. The meditations of Anselm or Aelred of Rievaulx, who are able to express their affections and longings in a practised way, moving easily from one idea to another, would have been literally unthinkable a century before. One might gather many examples of this sort: the skilful satire in which the individual voiced his protest against society, the lyric poetry in which he declared his personal desire, the intelligent political commentary of a man such as John of Salisbury, all depended equally on the achievement of sensitive and elegant literary forms. Erasmus, in the early sixteenth century, declared that we are nothing without Greek, *sine Graecitate*; it can certainly be said of the men of the twelfth century that they would have been nothing *sine Latinitate*. It was the indispensable preliminary for the discovery of the individual. At this point, indeed, we may observe a paradox. The twelfth century was not only the age of a brilliant (if short-lived) flowering of Latin literary culture. It was also the period when the vernacular languages of western Europe established themselves as important modes of literary expression. This does not reduce the importance which I have assigned to the recovery of a true and skilful Latinity. However much the national languages might have developed in the course of our period, they were not yet capable of performing the function of Latin. The world of learning in the twelfth century was very much an international one; monks belonged to orders with houses in many countries, scholars attended schools along with men of many nations. Of all the vernacular tongues, only Anglo-Saxon (so far as we know) had been used much before 1100 for purposes of learning and government; and Anglo-Saxon was doomed as a language by the long-term effects of the Norman Conquest. The leaders of the twelfth-century Renaissance were not, as a rule, contemptuous of languages other than Latin. Aelred of Rievaulx on his death-bed had an English phrase on his lips, "for Christ's love", but he wrote his books in Latin so as to address an international audience. Indeed, it might be argued convincingly that the Latin Renaissance did not impede, but actively assisted, the development of literature in the various national tongues.* The earliest Old French romances were stories of Greece or Rome, and Chrétien de Troyes, who raised the romance to a high level of artistry, had certainly had a sound education in the cathedral schools, and knew his Ovid. As to the emergence of the troubadour lyric, its origins are still a matter of much dispute, but one influence on it may well have been the work of composers (*tropatores*) of Latin verses for liturgical use. It is therefore reasonable, if at first surprising, to claim that the mastery of Latin composition was the most important contribution of humanism to the discovery of the individual. It made possible, for scholarly writers, a naturalness and immediacy of observation, and a subtlety of reflection, which had been impossible in previous centuries, and it assisted the development of vernacular literature, which at its best showed some of the same qualities.

Combined with this rather technical meaning of "humane letters", the word humanism also carries a more general significance. It expresses a sympathy with, and delight in, mankind; an idea expressed in Terence's famous line "I think nothing human foreign to myself". Such an interest in humanity was one of the dominant features of twelfth-century thought and literature, and will be extensively illustrated in this book. It is closely akin

* This is not to deny that the converse is also true. The natural ease of twelfth-century Latin was partly due to the influence of vernacular speech, which is evident in its style and constructions.

to a respect for the individual, since (in spite of the remarks of some cynics) it is difficult to have a high regard for humanity if one does not value individual men. It is significant that the word *humanitas*, which since about A.D. 600 had been used almost without exception in a pejorative sense to indicate human frailty, now recovered its former dignity. Bishop Ivo of Chartres at the beginning of the twelfth century employed it in its classical sense of philanthropy or kindness, and *humanus* once more came to carry a favourable connotation.[12] This delight in humanity was in most writers theologically directed. The grandeur of man lay in his divine vocation and calling, and in the possibilities of fellowship with God which lay open to him; and it may be found side by side, sometimes in the same author, with a deep sense of the sin and misery of the present human condition. Yet even this limitation must not be stressed too much. As we shall discover, there was a real interest in man as he actually *is*, which was seen as the starting-point of the glory to which he might rise. We are able to observe a fascination with individual experience which is often (although not always) seen within a Christian framework, but which does not discount the value of human activity even when it falls far short of the perfection which was the ultimate goal.

ORIGINS

The men of the twelfth century were conscious of looking back to the past, even to the far distant past, to find guidance in the problems which were confronting them, and we must therefore ask how far they discovered their interest in mankind and in the individual within the framework of the ideas which they found there. Above all, they turned to Christianity and to the classical past for guidance. It is at once obvious that the Western view of the value of the individual owes a great deal to Christianity. A sense of individual identity and value is implicit in belief in a God who has called each man by name, who has sought him out as a shepherd seeks his lost sheep. Self-awareness and a serious concern with inner character is encouraged by the conviction that the believer must lay himself open to God, and be remade by the Holy Spirit. From the beginning, Christianity showed itself to be an "interior" religion. It also contains a strong element of respect for humanity. Its central belief, that God became man for man's salvation, is itself an affirmation of human dignity which could hardly be surpassed, and its principal ethical precept is that a man must love others as he loves himself. The value of the individual and the dignity of man are both written large in the pages of the Scriptures. It is understandable that in the centuries before 1100 these convictions had made only a limited impact upon the primitive society of western Europe. It depended largely upon tradition, and therefore could give little scope to the individual, and, as we shall see later, social conditions were not such as to encourage a high view of human dignity. Yet, even in these unfavourable circumstances, the Church had maintained at least a silent witness to the humanist elements in the gospel. It is striking that in a Europe so predominantly agricultural, the Church maintained a liturgical year based not upon the cycle of seasons but upon the sacred history and the feasts of the saints, upon man and God's acts in man, thus preserving the belief that the key to the understanding of the world lay, not in the natural order, but in the history of man. Ultimately a Christian origin can be found for many of the elements in the European concept of the self.

Yet, if we turn to the Fathers and the writers of the New Testament, we find that their concept of personality qualified its stress upon the individual by the inclusion of some very important corporate elements. Jesus Christ was regarded not as another human being, separate from (although better and greater than) the believer. Saint Paul expresses his own experience in a quite different way: "I have been crucified with Christ; it is no longer I who live, but Christ who lives in me; and the life I now live in the flesh I live by faith in the Son of God, who loved me and gave himself for me" (Gal. 2.20). The boundaries have been broken between Christ and Paul. It is not the relationship of two personalities, but the indwelling of one in the other. Since the believer is identified with Christ, he is therefore identified also with all other believers: "There is neither Jew nor Greek, there is neither slave nor free, there is neither male nor female; for you are all one in Christ Jesus" (Gal. 3.28). The way was thus open for the community-language which is so characteristic of the New Testa-

ment. The Church is the body of Christ, each member a limb in it.
All believers share in the one Spirit, all are stones in the living
Temple. This element in early Christian thinking severely modifies
the strong individualism which we have also seen to be present,
but it has received relatively little attention in the Western
Church. The reasons are not far to seek. With the revival of
learning and personal devotion in the years after 1050, men seized
eagerly upon the message of individual salvation in ways which
will be examined later, but the language of community meant
less to them because it had arisen within a social situation so
foreign to their experience. In a Europe where every man was,
officially at least, a Christian, they could not be expected to enter
into the faith and love which had, long ago, bound together the
members of a small group, called to witness in a non-Christian
society. The words of the New Testament were of course revered,
but in so far as they related to the life of a tightly knit community,
they could no longer be understood in their original meaning.
There were, indeed, important exceptions to this generalization.
The monasteries, and especially the Cistercian houses, still
preserved something of the pattern of an early Christian Church:
a community of moderate size, united in a common experience
of conversion from the world and conscious of its own corporate
identity. It is therefore not an accident that the Cistercians were
more successful than any other group in uniting a contemporary
outlook with one which preserved many of the traditional elements.
For the Church in general the period from 1050 to 1150 was one of
great and far-reaching reconstruction and reform, but scarcely
any of these reforms increased the sense of community within
the local churches. Indeed, the whole tendency was to diminish
the sense of community. Two examples, of quite different kinds,
will illustrate this point. The Eucharist had been, for the early
Church, the supreme expression of its unity. By 1050 regular
communion by the people had become rare, but there was no
systematic attempt to restore it. The new practices which arose
in the celebration of the Mass, such as the elevation of the host,
were directed, not towards the restoration of community, but
towards the kindling of personal devotion. Again, under the
older canon law, the position of a bishop was safeguarded by the

rule that he could be deposed only by a synod of his colleagues. He was thus protected from injustice by recourse to the community of the local church. The canon lawyers of the twelfth century, however, turned to a quite different way of providing protection: appeal to Rome. The Church of the twelfth century thus saw a revival of personal piety, expressed in a variety of ways which we shall have to examine; but it failed to recover a sense of community for the faithful as a whole. The individual for the future was to be restricted, not by the mind of the local church, but by the authority of the hierarchy.

The second source of respect for the individual is probably to be found in the classical past. To summarize the role of the individual in Graeco-Roman civilization, within the framework of an introductory chapter, would obviously be impossible. It would also be useless for the purpose of our present subject, because large areas of the literature of Greece and Rome were entirely unknown to the men of the twelfth century. Indeed, the controversy whether it was proper for Christians to read the literature of the pagan past at all was still raging in the eleventh century, and was by no means settled in the twelfth. To a Cistercian such as Bernard of Clairvaux the inheritance of the classical past probably meant little. Quotations from classical authors are rare in his works, and nearly half of the entire total was included in the sermon to the clerks of Paris, for whose benefit Bernard had evidently worked up some appropriate passages. The twelfth century was inclined to help itself to what it wanted from classical literature, as the Hebrews had robbed the Egyptians of their jewels—an analogy which gave peace of mind to a number of uneasy consciences among the scholars of the time. None the less, the experiences of the classical age impinged upon the Middle Ages in a number of different ways, and it is therefore necessary to hazard some generalizations about the character of this influence. For a great part of the history of the Ancient World, traditional institutions remained strong, and inhibited interest in the person as distinct from his social group. The family, the city-state, and the tradition of reverence for Rome, all had this effect. There was, however, another aspect. The growth of great cities and vast areas of imperial government dissolved many of these traditional units. What Bolgar has called the

"later world of rabbit-warren towns and monster autocracies"[13]
led to the emergence of quite different cultural forms. One of these,
he rightly suggests, was "despair born of chaos". The individual
lost any hope of influencing the course of events; indeed, he was
deprived by imperial legislation even of the hope of changing his
position and status in society. The result was the development, at
various levels of sophistication, of religions of world-renunciation.
The initiates of such faiths were given the power to escape from
the confining shackles of the body and to find the hidden way to
mystical union with the One. Here we are far away from a concern
with the individual, as he has been understood in western Europe,
for all that makes up his life and his experiences was regarded as
irrelevant or even inimical to that liberation from the self which
was the goal of Neoplatonism or of the Manichees. On the other
hand, this dissolution of the older order could have a different
consequence which has been well explained by Alan Douglas:

> If, as has often been observed, the break-up of the classical
> system of internally close-knit independent "city-states" left
> the individual often bewildered and rudderless, at the same
> time it conferred new responsibilities and forms of ethical
> status. The frontiers are wider—and more like our own. For man
> confronts the universe not as a citizen but as an individual."[14]

The consequence, especially amongst the most highly privileged
groups in society, was the emergence of thoughts and feelings
which were both individual and humanist. Such a movement is
observable at Rome about 50 B.C., and its influence endured in
literary circles for a considerable time. The individual, freed
from the conventional ethics which had formerly governed his
actions, declared his desires in an outburst of lyric poetry; historians such as Sallust and later Suetonius reflected upon the motives
and characters of statesmen, although they were still inclined to
see them as types rather than as fully formed personalities.
Among the many interests of Cicero was counted a keen observation of personal relationships, delightfully illustrated in the
dialogues on Friendship and Old Age, which were extremely
popular in the Middle Ages. Cicero (although he was known only
through a very limited number of his works) and Seneca were,

for the men of the twelfth century, probably the most influential of the classical Roman writers, and it is interesting to observe that they were by disposition the most humanist of all, in that they saw an essential unity in mankind and even an equality of value among men. Thus Cicero could write: "There will not be different laws in Rome and in Athens, or different laws now and in the future, but all nations at all times will be under the sway of one law, everlasting and unchangeable."[15] Seneca even applied such ideas to slavery, that classical institution which to our eyes constitutes the ultimate denial of a humanist ideal: "they are slaves; or, rather, men".[16] The remarkable popularity of Seneca in later ages, however, did not depend so much on his humanism, as upon that vein of self-examination which is so evident a feature of his letters.[17] The conscious and patient pursuit of virtue; the profession of a desire for leisure and meditation, conducted amid a life of simplicity; the choice of a guide and mentor, after whose example we may fashion our own conduct and disposition; all this commended him greatly both to scholars and to monks in the twelfth century. Alan of Lille described him as *optimus excultor morum mentisque colonus*, and Godfrey of Saint Victor produced an even more remarkable couplet:

> To the counsels Lucilius from Seneca heard,
> The Gospel itself can be scarcely preferred.

To the modern reader of Seneca's letters the chasm which separates him from Christianity appears enormous. It is true that, in his measured way, he was concerned with self-examination and the pursuit of disciplined virtue. But there is no passion in Seneca; indeed, as he was a Stoic, his ideal of the interior life was the elimination of passion. Nothing could be further from the intense affection which, in twelfth-century ideals, bound the lover to Christ. Seneca knew friendship, but he cannot be said to have felt love, which (in any passionate sense) he would have regarded as an intrusion into his inner peace. Yet the gap between Seneca and the gospel was not evident in the Middle Ages. Even those who severely criticized some of his views did not perceive that his approval of suicide, for example, was not an unhappy aberration but was the key to his whole understanding of life. His Stoic calm and his cultivation of excellence of character were seen through Christian spectacles, and so were able to influence the age more than one would have thought possible.

This inclination to see Seneca as the fellow-traveller of Christ was part of a more general tendency to amalgamate classical culture and the doctrine of the Church. If some writers were hostile to any use of pagan authors, others defended their use on the ground that they were forerunners of the true revelation. It is convenient and logical from our standpoint to divide the influences upon the period from 1050 to 1200 into two, the Christian and the classical, but at the time this division was not clearly apparent, for by the very fact of its entry into Graeco-Roman civilization Christianity had become marked by its characteristic tendencies. The world-renunciation of the second and third centuries A.D. had influenced the Church deeply. The deserts of Egypt and Syria overflowed with hermits, in flight from, or in protest against, the great and luxury-loving cities of Antioch and Alexandria. From this root arose the monasticism of western Europe, which retained a clear line of communication with its past in the works of Cassian, whose account of the lives and sayings of the desert Fathers was prescribed for regular reading. At the same time the humanist tendencies of some Latin thinkers were also incorporated into Christian theology. Cassian himself was deeply influenced by Cicero's teaching on friendship, and Ambrose rewrote in Christian terms the *de Officiis* of Cicero. The massive works of Saint Augustine summed up many of the tendencies of both biblical and classical thought. His *Confessions* has some title to be regarded as the first auto-biography ever written. It is obviously a product of Christian experience and reflection, profoundly influenced by the Bible and especially by the works of Saint Paul, but to be fully understood it has also to be seen within the general tradition of self-exploration in the late Graeco-Roman world.[18] The *Confessions* may indeed be placed beside the great treatise *The City of God* as a critique, from the Christian point of view, of the philosophies which were popular in the Roman Empire in its declining years. The one recorded Augustine's personal involvement with them, and his slow movement towards Catholicism as the way of life and thought which most perfectly fulfilled his own longings: "For thou hast made us for thyself, and our heart is restless till it find rest in thee". The other is a more objective analysis of these systems of thought, in a major attempt to create a Christian philosophy of history. The *Confessions*, as we shall see, lay at the root of a good deal of medieval autobiography, and helped to establish the sense of the importance of each individual's experiences within the purposes of God. *The City of God* was the starting-point for much of the medieval thought about history, and may be counted a deeply humanist work, not in the sense that it sees the historical process as determined purely by human purposes (which it most certainly does not) but in the sense that it envisages the course of history as controlled by purposes which may be advanced by human participation, and which are in the long term designed for the salvation of man.

The mingling of Christian and classical traditions is to be found in an extreme form in the work of Boethius (*c.* 480–525), a writer little known in the modern world, but whose influence upon the culture of the twelfth century was profound.* Boethius formed the great ambition to translate into Latin the great corpus of Greek philosophy, which the West was in danger of losing because of the disappearance of the knowledge of Greek. He was able to fulfil only a tiny part of this plan, but to him the twelfth century owed a great deal of its slender knowledge both of Aristotle and of the Platonic tradition. From our point of view, by far his most interesting book was his last, *The Consolation of Philosophy*. This work has always provided a *cause célèbre* in the question of the continuity of Hellenistic and Christian ideas. On the one side, it contains the last reflections of a Catholic statesman, disgraced and imprisoned by the Arian ruler of Italy. As Boethius was soon to die at his hands, he could with justice be represented as a martyr for the

---

* The question of the personal beliefs of Boethius, and the character of his influence, has given rise to an abundant literature. The best and fullest examination is that of P. Courcelle, *La Consolation de Philosophie dans la tradition littéraire* (Paris, 1967). David Knowles is good on the extent of his influence (*The Evolution of Medieval Thought* (London, 1962), p. 53), but is perhaps inclined to exaggerate the readiness with which the book was accepted as a great Christian classic. There was a fairly general awareness in the twelfth century of the problems which it presented.

faith. On the other hand, it contains nothing that is specifically
Christian. Boethius is consoled by the rational reflections of
Philosophy, who expounds to him the wisdom offered by Greek
thinkers, especially those of the Neoplatonist school. The scholars
of the twelfth century were as fully aware of this paradox as those
of our own age, and they reacted in a variety of ways. Some condemned *The Consolation of Philosophy*, or at least expressed serious
reservations about it. Others welcomed it in spite of its philosophical content, and yet others regarded it as a great book precisely
because of its Platonizing tendencies. While it would therefore
be wrong to suggest that the twelfth-century thinkers were prepared to accept the book as a Christian classic, without considerable criticism, it undoubtedly provided a point of contact between
Christianity and the Greek past. Those inclined to philosophizing
could use it as a charter of liberties, and even the most conservative
were obliged to hesitate before rejecting the work of a great
Catholic who had died for his beliefs. It also helped to bring
them into touch with the classical approach to self-examination,
which we also observed in Seneca. The great body of the book
consists of a carefully reasoned consideration of the order of the
universe, but it is at the same time a personal work, composed
"while I was mutely pondering within myself, and recording
my sorrowful complaints with my pen".[19] The sovereign remedy
against ills is seen as true self-knowledge: "It is because
forgetfulness of thyself hath bewildered thy mind that thou
hast bewailed thee as an exile, as one stripped of the blessings
that were his."[20]

When the scholars of the twelfth century turned back to the
past, they therefore did not perceive a sharp contrast between their
Christian and classical inheritances. When they turned to Boethius,
to Cassian, to Augustine, to Ambrose, they read works which bore
the imprint of the Hellenistic world as well as of the New Testament. Combined with Christian insights, they could find some of
the humanism of Cicero and Seneca; a concern with friendship
which was immediately derived from Cicero; a self-examination
which showed some of the marks of classical tradition. Even those
with tender consciences, who refused to read the pagan authors,
imbibed something of the classical past at second hand, and bolder

spirits were encouraged to treat the classical authors as providing a preparation for the gospel. This was the varied tradition available to the men of 1100. We must consider now why they turned back to claim their inheritance.

2 The Background, 900–1050

Only a slender line of continuous tradition connects the learning of the Ancient World with that of the twelfth century. In the barbarian kingdoms which succeeded the Roman Empire in the west, classical culture survived only in fragments, for the knowledge of Greek disappeared almost completely, and even the major Latin authors were little read. We have seen that the triumph of Christianity provided a real continuity with Graeco-Roman culture, but the effects of this were not fully apparent for many centuries, because the Fathers (who had preserved some of the classical values), while being greatly revered, were only read to a limited extent and were even less understood. The Church became adjusted to the barbarian society in which it now lived. To call the western nations after A.D. 600 "barbarian" is not to insult them, but to describe them. They lived in a world largely without cities, for the cities of the west had never been as developed as those of the east, and had become smaller still as a result of political disorder and the reduction of trade. Outside Italy, only a steadily diminishing group could read and write, and literacy became increasingly the preserve of the clergy. The bonds of society were personal and tribal, and the idea of public authority progressively disappeared, to such an extent that early medieval Europe had no word corresponding to the *respublica* of the Roman world or to "state" in the modern age. It is therefore not surprising that some scholars have suggested that the western kingdoms of the Dark Ages must be considered on the analogy of primitive societies in other continents, and that the study of these societies will throw light on the development of western Europe.

It would be idle to deny that such similarities exist, but the comparison gives an even sharper point to our inquiry why western Europe developed a strong sense of the value of the individual, whereas western Africa did not. There is one very distinctive element in European history which has few parallels among other primitive societies: the barbarian nations of the Dark Ages were heirs to a complicated and sophisticated cultural tradition.[1] When circumstances were sufficiently advantageous, an attempt could be made to recover the learning of the past. For this reason the development of Europe from 500 to 1500 has been described as a pattern of three Renaissances—those of the Carolingian period, of the twelfth century, and of the fifteenth century.[2] Closer study, however, indicates that the process of exploring the riches of classical culture was not restricted to these three periods, for the wisdom of the Ancient World was the natural point of reference for a learned man at any time. Thus about A.D. 1000 Otto III placed on his seal the motto "Renewal of the Roman Empire", and he actively encouraged interest in the classical and Byzantine world. The "three Renaissances" are the times when the re-discovery of the classics and the Fathers made most progress and caused most excitement in the minds of contemporaries. The first of these, Charlemagne's ambitious attempt to achieve political unity and an extensive recovery of learning, was in ruins by 900, destroyed by internal dissension and the ravages of external enemies.

The tenth century has been described with some justice as the lowest point of European history. The West was the victim of waves of invasions coming from three sides. The Northmen were still ravaging Gaul; the Magyars carried out extensive raids in Germany and northern Italy, and were only finally repelled at the Battle of the Lech in 955; and the Saracens plagued the coasts of the Mediterranean, and even impeded traffic across the Alps. Amid such wretchedly unhappy social conditions one would not expect to find much optimism about man, nor respect for the individual; and as we shall see, despair of the human condition was in fact widespread. Yet there were also circles which were concerned with the preservation and ordering of society. Within the Church the tradition of Christian worship, and of ideas associated with it, was maintained, and there were two other centres which require our particular attention. The first is the court of the Ottonian Emperors, and the Churches which they administered. The coronation of Otto I as Emperor at Rome in 962 marked the establishment of German supremacy over a large part of Europe,

and Otto and his successors were concerned with the artistic
and liturgical expression of their dominance. The second centre
is to be found in the reformed monasteries. This reform found its
most famous expression in the foundation of Cluny in Burgundy
in 910, and gradually spread to many parts of Europe. The views
of the Cluniac reformers were expressed in a heightened form by a
series of Italian monks and hermits, who included some of the
most striking men of the time: Romuald (died 1027), friend of
Otto III; Peter Damiani (died 1072), adviser of the reforming
papacy; and John, abbot of Fécamp in Normandy (died 1078),
writer of popular and influential prayers. On the whole, imperial
court and monastic reformers co-operated warmly until after
1050, but their underlying attitudes differed sharply.

The ideas of the Ottonian court were rooted in traditional Christian symbolism, as it had been received in Germany, and especially
in a firm belief in the sovereignty of God and the victory of Christ.
These ideas continued to find expression in the liturgy of the
Church all over Europe, as in a famous Easter hymn written early
in the eleventh century and ascribed to Fulbert of Chartres:

> Ye choirs of new Jerusalem,
> Your sweetest notes employ,
> The Paschal victory to hymn
> In strains of holy joy.
>
> How Judah's Lion burst his chains,
> And crushed the serpent's head;
> And brought with him, from death's domains,
> The long-imprisoned dead.
>
> Triumphant in his glory now
> His sceptre ruleth all,
> Earth, heaven and hell before him bow,
> And at his footstool fall.[3]

Passion hymns celebrated the cross as a victory. They were
written mostly for the feast of the Holy Cross, and they stood
firmly in the steps of Venantius Fortunatus in the sixth century:

Sing, my tongue, the glorious battle,
Sing the ending of the fray;
Now above the Cross, the trophy,
Sound the loud triumphant lay:
Tell how Christ, the world's Redeemer,
As a Victim won the day.[4]

The depiction of the crucifix in art expressed this vision of the triumphant Christ. The crucifix of the time was very different from those to which we have become accustomed. Among some variations a fairly standard form can be perceived. Christ, clad in a loin-cloth, is nailed to the cross, watched by Mary and John and the bearers of spear and reed. Above the cross sun and moon veil their faces. The figure of Christ is alive and upright, feet side by side upon a support. His eyes are open, his arms straight, and he shows no sign of suffering. His face is often beardless and young.* It is a remarkable fact that in the first thousand years of the Church's history, years in which death was often close and threatening to most men, the figure of the dead Christ was almost never depicted. The crucifix was conceived as an expression of the triumph of Christ, the Lord of all things. Moreover, as we shall see in a later chapter, Christian tradition was uneasy about considering Christ as a suffering man, and preferred to see in him the expression of divine power. The Church had long before condemned as heretical the view, known as Docetism, that Christ's sufferings were merely apparent, but on the whole it preferred not to lay stress on this human aspect of the passion. It is true that at the end of the tenth century we find the first instances of a revolutionary type of crucifix which portrayed the Lord as dead, and which stressed his suffering and his mortality. Yet by 1050 the living-Christ tradition was still important, and in some places completely dominant. Long afterwards vivid examples were still being produced. To our eyes, trained in another tradition, some of these depictions of the living Christ are startling. He looks like a Greek god, Great Pan rather than the Man of Sorrows.[5]

The cross, then, was a divine victory. On this point, the Church

* Plates 5 and 7.

of the Dark Ages stood solidly in the footsteps of earlier centuries. When we ask how the fruits of this victory might be appropriated by the individual, we discover how deeply the thinking of the Church had been modified, both by the conversion of Europe and by the barbarization of European society. For the early Church, to become a Christian was a deliberate personal choice, involving both an interior change (repentance) and an exterior one (baptism and acceptance of Christ as Lord). Service of Christ thus consisted both of individual decision and of membership in a close community dedicated to fellowship and witness. As was noticed in the last chapter, neither of these experiences could be meaningful to the men of the tenth century. It required no personal choice to become a Christian, nor did the believer find himself to be part of a community distinct from society as a whole. In many ways, the conversion of Europe and its barbarization may be seen as part of the same process. That is not to say, as Gibbon thought, that the Christianity produced the barbarism, but rather that a primitive society normally finds it difficult to allow for individual decisions or for a variety of opinions, so that the multiplicity of religious views which marked the late Roman Empire was unable to endure in the new kingdoms of the west, and Christianity seized the opportunity of becoming the one accepted pattern of belief. To achieve this, the Church had to pay a high price in the loss of that balance between individual and community which had been the strength of the early Church. Religion was no longer a matter for personal decision, and the old community of love and fellowship was replaced by a quite different ideal of conformity to the norms accepted by society. In this situation it will be understood that tenth-century writers did not discuss the question how the victory of Christ was relevant to the individual, for it would not have presented itself to them as a problem. We can, however, observe several features in Carolingian and post-Carolingian thought which are relevant to the question.

Fundamental among these was a return to the Old Testament. The Church could no longer recognize itself in the small communities in the Graeco-Roman cities who had received the letters of Saint Paul, and found the godly kingdom of Israel more suited to its needs for a model.[6] There it could find a rural community, worshipping the one true God in obedience to his anointed king and defending its borders by incessant warfare. The world of David was more familiar than the world of the apostles. This reversion to Old Testament models obviously constituted a major revolution in the life and thinking of the Church. Perhaps its most obvious manifestation was the belief in the divinely ordained government of the world, in which the Emperor was God's representative. The Frankish realm was refounded in the eighth century upon a new theory of kingship, the Christian king being seen on the analogy of Davidic kingship, and being anointed like David.[7] This was very different from the thought of the early Church, which had seen Christ as the fulfilment of the kingship of David, and all believers as sharers in the kingship of Christ. Earthly rulers had to be obeyed, for they exercised a lawful dominion, but their authority was not conceived in anything like the way in which Charlemagne and his successors saw their power. "During the first seven centuries of our era, there was no Christian kingship properly so called."[8] The idea formulated by the Carolingians was taken up in a still more extreme form by their tenth-century successors in Germany, the Ottonians. They saw themselves as God's deputies on earth, a concept vividly expressed in ceremonies such as solemn crown-wearings and the *Laudes Regiae*. The monarch was seated in majesty, while the choir sang the praises of Christ and the king. Such rites immensely impressed contemporaries; at one of William the Conqueror's crown-wearings, a by-stander was so overcome that he cried out, "Behold, I see God".[9] Otto III (983–1002) was on one occasion depicted in the *mandorla*, the symbol of divinity which usually surrounded the glorified Christ. A poem of about A.D. 1000 described Otto in his role of representative of Christ. "Strong in war, mighty in peace, yet mild in both; among triumphs, war and peace alike, he always considered his poor folk, and so is called Father of the Poor."[10] A prominent churchman could describe Conrad II in 1024 as the vicar of Christ.[11] There is something splendid about this vision of world order, but it was a way of thinking essentially primitive, expressed through rites and symbols, and containing relatively little of reason and reflection. It also gave little place to the individual, whose role was never elaborated but implicitly was confined to accepting his position in this hierarchically ordered society.

It is, however, at once necessary to qualify this conclusion. The monarchs of the period 900–1050 expressed their divinely given authority in imposing rituals, but they did not possess the civil service or professional army which would have been needed for the establishment of despotism, or even of an efficient central-ized government. Their success rested on their personal qualities, and especially on their ability to command the loyalty of their followers. Victory in war, combined with generosity and faithful-ness to his warrior nobles, were above all the things which made a successful ruler. It was an intensely personal society,* in which what we would regard as normal administrative processes were dependent on the individual's qualities of justice and courage. *The Song of Roland* provides us with a nice example. All the members of Charlemagne's court knew of Ganelon's treason, but it was impossible to condemn him for it until the king could find a champion brave enough to challenge Pinabel, Ganelon's kinsman and advocate, to a judicial duel. Admittedly, this episode was only recorded at the end of the eleventh century, but everything goes to show that it was a correct reflection of French judicial practice, then and earlier. Odo of Cluny, early in the tenth century, had written a life of Gerard of Aurillac, to hold him up as an example of mercy and justice. It is abundantly clear that simple public order, let alone enlightened administration, depended entirely on the personal qualities of the nobles, who could rarely be disci-plined if they were extortionate or violent. In this sense the attitude of the individual was all-important, and the conditions already existed which were to produce codes of chivalrous conduct and an intense interest in individual characteristics. The concept of the divinely anointed king therefore did not efface personal qualities, which remained of paramount importance for the functioning of society.

The divine ordering of human society was also made manifest,

* The ambiguous standing of the individual has been examined by L. Génicot in a brief but perceptive paper, "Valeur de la personne ou sens du concret", in *Miscellanea Mediaevalia in memoriam Jan Frederik Niermeyer* (Groningen 1967), pp. 1–8.

for the men of the time, in the liturgy of the Church. As in many primitive societies, great importance was attached to ritual. At Cluny, the greatest monastic centre of the tenth and eleventh centuries, the liturgy was so expanded in length and complexity that it swallowed up much of the time originally allotted to study and to manual labour. The kings and nobility were concerned to maintain the performance of the monastic ritual, to the extent that the government of the time has been described with justice as "the liturgical state". These were the years, moreover, in which the construction of great stone churches was begun, far surpassing anything previously known in northern and western Europe, and more elaborate than the basilicas which the Church had required in the late Roman Empire. The monasteries in particular used their wealth to provide buildings and treasures on a scale appropriate to the splendid performance of the liturgy. In all this the part of the individual was reduced to participating in, or to witnessing, the solemn re-enactment of God's victory in Christ. This is expressed in a Carolingian hymn which is still well known in the modern Church:

> The people of the Hebrews
> With palms before thee went;
> Our praise and prayer and anthems
> Before thee we present.
>
> To thee before thy passion
> They sang their hymns of praise;
> To thee now high exalted
> Our melody we raise.[12]

A sequence, or verse, written by Wipo in the early eleventh century, contains the same invitation to the worshippers to behold, and rejoice in, the re-enactment of the divine victory:

> Christians, to the Paschal Victim
> Offer your thankful praises!
> A Lamb the sheep redeemeth:
> Christ, who only is sinless,
> Reconcileth sinners to the Father;
> Death and life have contended

In that combat stupendous:
The Prince of Life, who died, reigns immortal.

Speak Mary, declaring
What thou sawest wayfaring:
"The Tomb of Christ, who is living,
The glory of Jesu's Resurrection:
Bright angels attesting,
The shroud and napkin resting.
Yea, Christ my hope is arisen:
To Galilee he goes before you."

Happy they who hear the witness, Mary's word believing
Above the tales of Jewry deceiving.
Christ indeed from death is risen, our new life obtaining.
Have mercy, victor King, ever reigning![13]

The simplicity of Wipo's words, and their direct appeal to the
faith of the hearer, warn us that something more was involved
than the recital of a liturgy which had an objective or magical
virtue of its own. The externals of the system call to mind the
role of religion in such a civilization as that of the Aztecs: the
concern of society to maintain the unceasing performance of the
liturgy, the huge buildings provided by communities which can
scarcely find the bare necessities of life for the peasantry, the
conduct of ritual in a language comprehensible only to a select
minority. While it is right to stress the primitive character of this
concern with ritual, an important qualification must be made.
The Church of the time liked to contrast the animal sacrifices
of the Temple with the unbloody sacrifice of praise offered by the
monastic order. The Aztec sacrifices, of human hearts plucked
from the living victims, would have shocked even the brutal
aristocracy of the early eleventh century; we are faced once again
with the paradox of a barbarian society which had access to a
humane cultural inheritance. However much the Church became
adjusted to the practices of contemporary society, it never came
to regard the attitude of the worshipper as a matter of indifference.
If in one sense its services had become more incomprehensible,
with the disappearance of Latin as a vernacular language, in other

ways the ceremonial was being popularized. This is particularly true of the appearance, perhaps from the tenth century onwards,* of simple plays representing the discovery of the empty tomb at Easter, the coming of the Magi at the Epiphany, and the Palm Sunday procession. In the Epiphany play priests representing the Magi visited Herod, in one part of the church, and the culminating moment came when a curtain was drawn back to reveal a statue of Virgin and child in majesty, manifested for the adoration at once of the Magi and of the congregation. These plays are interesting, not only because they bring us close to the origins of the dramatic tradition of the West, but also because they combine two themes. On the one hand, the adoration of a statue of the Virgin in majesty, and the honours which were normally paid to these statues, are part of the cultic observance of a primitive society. At the same time, these enactments of the Gospel story helped to bring the people close to the human Jesus in his lifetime. If we bear in mind the fact that the "dying-Christ" form of the crucifix had appeared in Germany shortly before A.D. 1000, we may not be far wrong in concluding that the roots of the devotion to the historical Jesus are to be found in a period considerably before 1050. It is true that literary evidence of personal devotion to the crucified Lord is slight before the late eleventh century, but the beginnings of this new devotion, which produced the fine prayers of Saint Anselm and Aelred, may go back a long way. Similarly, the years before 1050 saw a marked development in the devotion to relics and in pilgrimages to visit them, and here again we have the double aspect of cultic reverence ("Have you not gold and silver boxes full of dead men's bones?" asked William Rufus (1087–1100)) and of admiration for great human beings. The combination of an adoration which appears almost idolatrous with a respect for the humanity of Christ, the Virgin and the saints, may seem to us an odd one, but it is understandable in the

* The date of the emergence of these plays is disputed. In the text, I follow the views of I. H. Forsyth, "Magi and Majesty: a study of Romanesque Sculpture and Liturgical Drama", *Art Bulletin* 50 (1968) p. 215, where references to recent discussions may be found. The later development of the devotion to the crucified Jesus is considered in a subsequent chapter, pp. 139–144 below.

circumstances of the day. The Church had lost contact with the experiences of the New Testament, which presupposed a witnessing and small band of brethren. In part consciously and in part unconsciously, it offered Christ to the people in the simple forms in which they could apprehend him: both in association with statues and other cultic objects, and by a sharing in his human experiences as displayed in the liturgical plays. The affection for the historical Jesus did not receive its richest expression until the days of the twelfth-century Renaissance, but it should perhaps be regarded as a product of the dark period before the Renaissance itself had begun.

The imperial court and the liturgical tradition of the Church both proclaimed the kingship of Christ over this world. Although the monastic reformers worked closely with the imperial court, they had a different attitude. Our immediate impression, on reading the works of the Cluniacs and of the Italian hermits, is of an overwhelming tendency towards world-renunciation. Volumes could be filled with the passionate rejection of secular society by these writers, but one example may do service for all.* The biographer of Abbot Odo of Cluny, who died in 942, told of the capture of Odo's nephew as a small baby by a party of raiding Northmen near Tours. His nurse succeeded in escaping with the child, and brought him to Odo: "As soon as the boy was brought to our father he had him baptized, and raising his eyes to heaven prayed that he should die, and three days later the child gave up his spirit to heaven. His father became a monk."[14] In this success story modern values are reversed, and death in infancy, provided it is after baptism, is seen as the greatest happiness. Behind this

---

* This element has been stressed in a series of studies by R. Bultot, who has demonstrated that it was not merely important in the eleventh century, but was a lasting feature of medieval culture. I do not discuss it at length, partly because it is not the subject of this book, but also because it seems to me, as I have tried to explain, that the spirit of world-rejection coexisted with a positive affirmation of individual and humane values. The issue is considered in R. Bultot, *Christianisme et valeurs humaines. La doctrine du mépris du monde en Occident, de saint Ambroïse à Innocent III, t.IV: XIᵉ siècle* (Louvain 1963–4), and in J. Batany, "L'Eglise et le 'mépris du monde' ", *Annales, Economies, Sociétés* XX (1965), p. 1006.

way of thinking there lay a long tradition of monastic withdrawal from the world, but there is no doubt that many of the leading reformers were men sensitive to the conditions prevailing about them. It was an age of great poverty and insecurity, in which the Church was open to exploitation by a brutal military aristocracy, and in which violence had largely taken the place of law. Saint Romuald was driven to withdraw to a hermitage when his father killed a neighbour in a dispute over land, and it can readily be appreciated that outstanding men despaired of the human condition. We are in our own age familiar with the phenomenon of the "drop-out", who refuses to continue in society because he will not pay the price of conformity with the dominant attitudes. In the unhappy world of the tenth century withdrawal seemed to many perceptive men the only path to salvation. Their despair is expressed in the view, generally accepted until about 1100, that man had been created in order to make up the number of the fallen angels. This may seem to us no more than an idle fable, but it contains the important assumption that man's purpose is not human, but angelic; not to realize his true self, but to become something quite different.

We might reasonably conclude that in so bleak a landscape we may expect neither confidence in humanity nor interest in the individual, but such a conclusion would be false. Peter Damiani in the middle years of the eleventh century expressed a hatred for the world which was extreme and at times pathological, but he also thought that the purpose of renouncing the world was precisely to know oneself in one's own true being. Perhaps in a society so barbaric, so tied by the demands of kin and lord, it was only possible for the individual to discover himself by means of an exaggerated rejection of the outside world. This, at least, is the purpose of Damiani's writing:

> Let it cease then; let sterile attention to business cease. To indulge in fruitless labour is pointless. Let the mind return within itself, with all its resources collected. Let it gird itself attentively for the struggle against tireless enemies.[15]

So emphatic was Damiani about this that he expressed the hope that after death he would enter "the splendour of the inner

country."[16] One cannot readily imagine a more vivid statement of
that sense of "inwardness" which has already been defined as an
important element in individuality. Nor was Damiani alone in
this. About 1070 there was inscribed on the doorway of the church
of Sant' Angelo in Formis, "You'll climb to heaven if you know
yourself".[17] In those circles which were most strongly committed
to withdrawal from the world there was a keen interest in self-
exploration. It would indeed be scarcely too much to describe the
eremitical movement as a revolt of individuals against a constrict-
ing society. A man's life was normally dictated by the group within
which he was born; his ideals and standards would be those of his
class, his loyalties those of his lord and his family, and he would
have little choice but to follow the calling in life to which his
birth appointed him. One of the few other possibilities was offered
by the monastic reformers, who placed before men (or at least
before those with some elementary education) a way of life very
different from that of secular society, and invited them to choose it
in preference to the standards which they had inherited. From
an early date Cluny was not content to provide for children brought
up within the monastery, but admitted men from outside either as
full monks or (if they had insufficient education) as lay brothers.
The reformers, therefore, raised a question of values, and raised
it in the radical form of urging sympathizers to join them in their
rejection of the attitudes of aristocratic society. It thus offered
the individual a choice which challenged his loyalties at a deep
level. It is interesting to find that the "converts", those who
decided to make the break, provided the occasion for some of the
early experiments in biography and autobiography: Peter Damiani
wrote a life of Romuald; the life of Odo of Cluny includes a short
autobiographical section, describing his conversion in his own
words; and the first major autobiographical work, that of Otloh
of Saint Emmeram, was directly produced by a crisis of vocation,
although as we shall see, by 1032, when Otloh was in his agony
of hesitation, the issues were becoming more complex. It is not
too much to say that in the tenth century the monastic reformers
offered to the aristocracy the one alternative way of life and system
of values, and that through this conflict of roles some outstanding
men found themselves as individuals.

So far we have been concerned with the large principles and grand ideals entertained by the imperial court and the reformed monasteries. It is also relevant to our inquiry to learn something about the attitudes of ordinary men before 1050, but here, even if we confine ourselves to the aristocracy, we encounter an acute problem of evidence. Little remains in any language other than Latin, which is predominantly the vehicle for hymns, panegyrics, and exhortations. It would be very unwise to conclude from the absence of much surviving vernacular poetry that it was not being composed. On the whole it is likely that there was a great deal, both of lyric and epic poetry, especially in the Germanic languages. Provençal and French, being by origin popularized forms of Latin, must have begun later as instruments for composition, but it is probable enough that a good deal had been composed in both these languages by 1050.[18] Much of it may be highly relevant to the discovery of the individual, and it is conceivable that the troubadours received some of their most characteristic attitudes from predecessors unknown to us. One must simply concede that there is a serious gap in the evidence, and in an area where all is hypothesis it is useless to venture deeply. Nevertheless, it is possible to reach a few cautious conclusions.

Between the years 900 and 1050 it is probable that one of the favourite relaxations of the aristocracy was to listen to epic poems, narrating the glories and tragedies of former heroes. From the limited idea we can form of these* it is clear that aristocratic society was rigid in its ideals, and allowed little scope for individual initiative. A man had a few simple obligations prescribed by

---

* There is much dispute about the reliability of our sources of information. In the text, I have assumed that the *Waltharius* is a fairly accurate rendering (of very uncertain date, perhaps *c.* 930) of a German original, and that the older elements of the *Nibelungenlied* can be distinguished with reasonable confidence from the later "chivalric" ones. I have also assumed that the French epics written down in the twelfth century contained substantial amounts of older, traditional material. Even if these assumptions are accepted, we at once run into further uncertainties. The subtle handling of the Roland–Oliver relation may be a very late element in the poem, belonging rather to the atmosphere of twelfth-century humanism, and the inconsistency of the characters in the *Nibelungenlied* is perhaps the result of the clumsiness of its "chivalric" rewriting in *c.* 1200.

convention: to his lord, his kin, and his friend. Even friendship
was not a matter of personal inclination, but was a formal obligation entered upon by oath to the comrade or *compainz*. Such pairs
of friends were common in the poetry of the time, the most famous
of all being Roland and Oliver in *The Song of Roland*. Although
society was so conventional, we have already seen that it was also
intensely personal. The obligations of man and lord were so
binding that the character of each mattered enormously, and the
story of the epic tragedies usually turned either on a conflict
between two sworn loyalties or on the relationship between an
unworthy lord and his man. In *Waltharius* Hagen is torn between
his sworn friend Walter and his unworthy lord, the King of the
Franks, while the savage French epic *Raoul of Cambrai* is a tragic
study in loyalty and disloyalty: Raoul is driven to violence and
cruelty by his disinheritance by the incompetent King Louis,
and his brutality then poses an acute problem of obedience to
his own follower, the faithful Bernier. It would be a mistake to
look for great subtlety of observation of character in these epics,
and in some of them, such as the *Nibelungenlied*, the characters are
notably inconsistent in their actions.[19] The poets favoured, not so
much an analysis of character, as a set-piece or formal confrontation
between the leading actors. The friendship and conflict between
"the valiant Roland and wise Oliver" is one of the great episodes
of European literature, both for its delicate presentation of their
relationship and for the success with which each is made to represent
a distinct attitude to life. A modern man is likely to support the
cautious Oliver against proud Roland, who would not sound his
horn to summon help lest "in fair France my fame should suffer
scorn", but to the first hearers the issue would have been less clear.

The general tone of the epics was one of dignity and formality,
and they offered little scope for the portrayal of the more intimate
emotions. The women who figured in the earlier epics were
apparently those who were admired for their ability to support their
husbands and to administer their lands in a crisis; the interest
lay in the capable matron rather than in the young beauty. Roland's
unfortunate fiancée appears only at the very end of the poem, and
her sole function is to lament him inconsolably. The *Waltharius*
contains several fine scenes between Walter and his betrothed,

Hildegund, but they are not much concerned with the portrayal of inner feelings, and the relationship between the two is strikingly different from that prescribed in the twelfth-century poems of courtly love:

> At length the girl knelt on the ground and spoke:
> "Wherever you appoint, my lord, I'll go,
> And all you order I will gladly do."[20]

We would naturally turn to the lyric poetry of the time for the expression of more intimate emotions, but here, for most of western Europe, the evidence is even worse than for the epics. Irish and Icelandic verse, of which a certain amount survives, indicate that tenth-century man was not a stranger to delicate and private feelings, and warn us that the absence of such passages from the epics may be due to the character of these poems as formal tragedies. There is, for example, a moving Icelandic lament by a father on his son's death, and there are indications that the emotion of hopeless adoration for the beloved was also present in their poetry: "I cannot withhold my overwhelming love for the radiant mistress of the keys."[21] If we had more of this early vernacular verse, we might be less surprised by the apparently revolutionary appearance of "romantic" love in the twelfth century. It is certainly interesting to discover that, whereas we know of almost no love poetry in Latin during the Carolingian Renaissance, the period 900–1050 does leave us a little. One such poem is *Iam dulcis amica venito*,[22] uncertain in its metre and exact meaning, but moving in its delicacy and exciting in its promise for the future, for it shows a combination of Ovid and the Song of Songs, and an overlap between profane and sacred love, which we shall meet again in the twelfth century. It was, indeed, used as a hymn with only minor changes.

Alone in the wood I was hiding,	*Ego fui sola in silva*
And in secrecy I was abiding;	*et dilexi loca secreta;*
I fled from the crowded places,	*frequenter effugi tumultum*
And avoided the tumult of faces.	*et vitavi populum multum.*
Beloved, no longer delay,	*Karissima, noli tardare;*
Let us love one another today.	*studeamus nos nunc amare:*

Without you there is no delight;   *sine te non potero vivere;*
Now in love let us fully unite.   *iam decet amorem perficere.*

Iam decet amorem perficere. It was to be almost the theme song
of the new age.

The fitful survival of evidence should make us cautious in our
verdict on the years between 900 and 1050. We have noticed that
in many respects it was an age which offered little scope to the
individual and did not value individuality. The structure of
society was hierarchical, with the divinely authorized ruler at its
head; the worship of the Church was directed to the maintenance
of liturgy and ritual in prescribed forms; and many of the finest
minds of the age had despaired of human possibilities in this
world. Paradoxically, we have found that each of these attitudes
was not, on close investigation, as anti-individualist and anti-
humane as it appears at first sight. Actual government depended
almost completely on the loyalty and courage of the upper nobility;
the Church was at pains to involve the people in the re-enactment
of the central mysteries of Christ's life, death, and resurrection;
and the monastic reformers withdrew from society in order to
cultivate the possibilities of their own inner selves. While, therefore, the period was emphatically not one in which there was any
obvious confidence in man or in the individual, there existed under
the surface the possibility of a discovery of the individual. For
this potential to be realized formidable barriers would have to
be removed. The general level of learning was so low that it was
difficult to exchange ideas, or even to formulate them clearly.
The individual was caught up within a network of loyalties, with
little choice about his way of life or opportunity to select his own
values, and his only way of escape lay in the radical decision to
reject the world and retire to a monastery. Before there could be a
discovery of the individual, there would have to be a great increase
in learning and an enrichment of social possibilities and fluidity.
By 1050 both of these were beginning.

3 New Learning in a New Society

Greece had the first renown in chivalry and learning.
Then came chivalry to Rome, and and the heyday of
learning, which is now come into France.
CHRÉTIEN DE TROYES

A SOCIETY IN TRANSFORMATION

From the discussion so far, a relatively simple pattern has emerged. In the tradition which lay behind the medieval West, Christianity and classicism had assigned to the individual a high value, and stressed the virtue of self-knowledge. Germanic society itself depended, not on institutions, but on personal loyalties, and was therefore potentially fertile ground for an interest in the individual and in his relations with others. Once there was a growth in learning and a deeper understanding of the Bible, the Fathers, and the classics, all the pre-conditions for a major discovery of the individual would be present. Unhappily, the paths of history are rarely as clear as this, and the circumstances in which the discovery of the individual took place were much more complicated than this analysis indicates. The development of learning, when it took place, was part of a much wider transformation of society, and to understand it we must first examine this rapid change. This is not to say that the social and economic circumstances were the "cause" and the new learning the "effect", for the skills acquired through better education were themselves important in altering the conditions in which society lived; but, as far as they may be distinguished, it is convenient to examine first the wide perspectives of changing social conditions, and subsequently the revolution in learning: the twelfth-century Renaissance.

One change which is immediately apparent to the historian is the growth of the cities.* In the years before 1050, the cities

* The character of economic and social changes in the century after 1050 is still under discussion by historians, but there would be general

had been an insignificant part of Western society, except in Italy. Thereafter, growing opportunities for commerce not only stimulated a revival in the decayed cities of northern Italy, but brought into being a city civilization in Flanders and the Low Countries. The prosperity of the burghers of Flanders was built upon the manufacture of cloth; by the early twelfth century they were influential enough to demand extensive liberties, and they had become a major power in the politics of the area. They stood at the centre of an extensive network of commercial exchange. Flemish cloth was exported as far as Italy, and the cities themselves depended increasingly on the wool of England and the corn and wine of the Seine valley. The heavy, four-wheeled carts rumbling across the great chalk plain between Paris and Bruges are a symbol of the new economic order, as the corn fleets from Alexandria and Carthage had once represented the old, Mediterranean order of Rome. Flanders was, however, only an extreme case of a general development: the French cities also grew rapidly. Paris soon became the largest city north of the Alps, and the reasons for its expansion exemplify those which were operating in many parts of Europe. It was an important centre of communications, since the River Seine was itself a major highway for trade from east to west, and Paris was one of the few points at which it was bridged. It therefore became a place of resort both for merchants and pilgrims, who were further encouraged by the rich store of relics at the cathedral of Notre Dame and the abbey church of Saint-Denis. Its famous schools attracted students in large numbers from all over Europe, and in the course of the century the French kings increasingly made Paris their normal place of residence, thus

agreement that the period saw a great increase in the size of cities and the development by the aristocracy of new patterns of local control. The questions under dispute are the extent to which the leap forward in the late eleventh century rested on a sub-structure of agrarian and commercial development going far back into the Frankish period, and the extent of the damage done to the economy of northern France by Viking depredations. As these issues are not of immediate importance for my subject, I have not discussed them. The rival points of view may be found briefly set out in G. Duby and R. Mandrou, *A History of French Civilization* (London 1964), pp. 60–7, and A. R. Bridbury, "The Dark Ages", *Econ. Hist. Rev.* 22 (1969), pp. 526–37.

further increasing the importance and size of the city. A visitor of the late twelfth century, Guy de Bazoches, left a vivid pen-portrait:

> I am in Paris, in that royal city where abundance of natural wealth not only holds those who live there, but also attracts those from afar. Just as the moon outshines the stars in brilliance, so does this city, the seat of the monarchy, lift her proud head above the rest. She lies in the embrace of an enchanting valley, surrounded by a crown of hills which Ceres and Bacchus make fruitful. The Seine, proud river of the East, runs there a brimming stream, and holds in its arms an island which is the head, the heart, the marrow of the whole city. Two suburbs extend to right and left, of which the lesser alone rivals many cities. Each of these suburbs communicates with the island by two bridges of stone; the Grand Pont towards the north, on the side of the English Channel, and the Petit Pont towards the Loire. The first—great, rich, trading—is the scene of seething activity; innumerable ships surround it, filled with merchandise and riches. The Petit Pont belongs to the dialecticians, who walk there deep in argument. In the island, by the side of the King's palace that dominates the whole city, is seen the palace of philosophy, where study reigns as sole sovereign in a citadel of light and immortality.[1]

We do not know the population of these newly developed cities, but it is likely that, by modern standards, most of them were very small. What matters is not their absolute size, but the enormous increase which they represented in opportunities for hearing news and discussing ideas. Together with the pilgrim traffic which helped to encourage their growth, they provided the basis of the financial resources which made possible both the Gothic cathedrals and cathedral schools of high quality. They also encouraged the appearance of a more radical monasticism, inspired by the example of the desert Fathers. No doubt those who had known Alexandria or Antioch of old would not have been much impressed by Bruges, or even by Paris, but these new communities were still large enough to be alarming, and to set up the cry, "back to the wilderness", for now there was something to run away from:

"I will not dwell in cities, but rather in deserts and uncultivated places."[2] The cities proved to be centres of unrest. In the *burgenses* or rich bourgeoisie, and to an extent in the skilled craftsmen on whom industry depended, there were laymen, effective and to some degree both rich and leisured, who were unwilling to accept exclusion from power in secular and ecclesiastical matters. Below them was a proletariat, whose working conditions were at the mercy of the demand on the market, and the area of unrest was increased by the impact of the cities on the surrounding country-side (the *contado* as it was known in Italy), the traditional economy of which was disrupted in order that it might be directed into supplying the needs of the citizens. The turmoil expressed itself in a series of upheavals, among which were mingled demands for a commune and other civic liberties, support for the more radical wing of the movement for Church reform, and the encouragement of heretical preachers.

We must not work the cities too hard as an explanation for the changes which were taking place from 1050 onwards. The aristo-cracy itself was being transformed in its structure and its patterns of behaviour, although it is necessary to be cautious in describing this development because of the limited evidence available from the preceding period. Fundamentally two processes were at work. On the one hand, the lords were securing more effective control of their local areas. The obvious symbol of the new order was the castle. Wooden castles were widespread in eleventh-century France, and in the twelfth century those who could afford it replaced them with stone. Whoever held the castle enjoyed military control of the region. Meanwhile, the general breakdown of royal authority which had taken place in France in the tenth century had left local lords free to develop their own pattern of exploitation. This was based on their possession of very wide jurisdiction (*haute justice*) over their peasantry, and on a whole series of profitable rights: monopoly over the sale of salt and wine, monopoly of milling, and the right to take arbitrary levies and tallages. The expansion of agriculture at the same time assisted the new lordship, making possible the colonization of waste land and the clearance of forests, which the lord sponsored to his own profit. The dominance of the local family was further secured by the increasing tendency of estates to become hereditary, and to descend without division to the eldest son. The twelfth century saw the triumph of primogeniture as the normal rule of succession both in England and France, where indeed it had been developing for some considerable time. Well before 1200 there had appeared the pattern which was to endure until at least the eighteenth century, of local "great families", exercising wide rights over their peasantry and continuing in control of the neighbourhood for generations. This introduces us to the second change in the period, the tendency of the nobility to become an hereditary group separate from the rest of society. One element in this was the increasing importance and expense of cavalry warfare. Even before the year 1000, in parts of France the word *miles* had lost its general sense of a warrior, and had come to mean a man rich enough to possess a warhorse and the necessary equipment. By about 1100 the knightly class had become almost an hereditary group, and to say of the son of a noble that he was "not a knight" normally meant that he was still only a boy.[3] During the twelfth century the growing expense of cavalry equipment and the increasing elaboration of the ceremony of knighting tended to widen the gap between the knight, who occupied an honourable position within society, and the mercenary, who served for pay. The hereditary character of the noble caste at this time must, indeed, not be exaggerated. Twelfth-century society was far from being ossified, and it was still possible for a man of intelligence or military skill to win his way into the charmed circle of chivalry, and still more possible to rise to prominence within this society. Lothar of Supplinburg, born the heir to a small Saxon county, lived to be German Emperor from 1125 to 1137, and William Marshal rose by his prowess as a knight to become Earl of Pembroke and the most respected statesman of England. But the exceptions prove the rule: both of these entered the highest circles of the nobility by marriage, adopted by an establishment which appreciated their qualities.

The emergence of this new pattern of lordship did not necessarily bring with it the fragmentation of society into very small units. This was indeed its immediate effect in France, where between 1050 and 1100 large parts of the country lay at the mercy of little local lords, secure in their castles and dominating their neighbourhoods. In the long run the upper nobility enjoyed the benefit, for the development of the stone castle and of more effective and costly military equipment gave the initiative to those families who controlled resources sufficient to afford them. These developments took place at various times in different countries. They usually began in France, perhaps because the old order there had collapsed more completely than in England and Germany. Castles, for example, were common in eleventh-century France, were introduced into England after the Norman Conquest, and appeared in Germany on a large scale from the 1070s onwards. A similar pattern may be observed in most of the social changes which we have been considering. For this reason the new aristocracy is found in its most vigorous and self-confident form in France and Normandy. The names French or Frankish were increasingly used for the inhabitants of that area, covering what is now the northern half of France, who were French-speaking, and the Normans, at least between 1050 and 1150, usually counted themselves as French. The international power of this aristocracy was founded upon its great military effectiveness, which was admitted even by those who hated and feared it—the Byzantines were eager to employ Frankish mercenaries, and it was said with awe that a Frank on horseback would go through the walls of Babylon.[4] The widespread conquests achieved by this noble class obviously rested upon its courage and skill in battle. The First Crusade was largely a Franco-Norman enterprise, and the men of the duchy of Normandy overran England, southern Italy and Sicily, and Antioch. The international connections of these nobles were remarkable. Bohemond, one of the most striking figures of the early twelfth century, was a younger member of the Norman family which had established itself in power in southern Italy. In a stormy career he campaigned more than once against the Byzantines in the Balkans, visited Constantinople, fought the Turks in Anatolia, became Prince of Antioch, and visited France. At a slightly less exalted level we find international affiliations no less impressive: on the death of Robert of Rhuddlan, who had conquered a considerable part of north Wales, his brother came to fetch his body for burial in Normandy, and then continued to southern Italy to collect funds from other members of the family to provide a memorial.[5] The attitude of some of these nobles may be discerned from the story of the crusading leader who remained seated in the presence of the Byzantine Emperor. Alexius angrily demanded the man's name, but received the reply: "I am a Frank of the highest nobility." No more needed to be said, for no title could be greater.[6]

This aristocracy, which was redrawing the map of Europe and altering its society, naturally impinged also on its culture. At the beginning of the twelfth century we find for the first time, within the limits of our knowledge, the courts of the lay nobility becoming major centres of patronage. Adela, Countess of Blois, was in touch with many of the leading scholars and poets of northern France, and further south the courts of such men as William Count of Poitiers were becoming centres of troubadour songwriting. We shall have occasion later to examine in more detail the literature produced in these centres, but it can be said immediately that during the twelfth century it displayed three features, which corresponded with the interests of the aristocracy. It provided (in the elaboration of codes of chivalry) a purpose and ethic fitted to the new way of life; it contained a great deal about battle and prowess; and it was interested in heroic individuals and personal relations, as was fitting for a class whose position depended on personal valour and the ties between man and man. The picture is complicated, however, by the appearance within the aristocracy of two groups with special interests. One of these is that of the young men, the *iuvenes*, who spent some years in absence from their fathers' estates.[7] It is not clear how far this group is a new social phenomenon, or whether it had always existed, but without having, as far as we know, the same cultural impact. It is reasonable to think that the increasing adoption of primogeniture helped to bring such groups into existence, for it made it urgently necessary for younger brothers to find a wife and landed estates, as they could not hope for much from their father's inheritance. Moreover, the increasingly good political order in many parts of Europe made it less necessary to have sons in residence to defend the family estates, and obliged those who wanted adventure to seek it elsewhere, in tournaments, on crusade, or in areas where warfare was endemic. Whatever the origin of this group, its social and cultural significance was considerable. Socially it proved a mixing-point where landless knights, or even mercenaries, might meet men of high family and secure themselves patrons. Some young nobles made it a point of pride to entertain knights of this sort, thus making themselves a name for chivalric splendour and creating centres of political unrest; such a man was the young Henry, eldest son of Henry II of England. *The History of William the Marshal* is a real-life romance of a knight who rose to influence by securing the patronage of the Plantagenets. Culturally, such young men, who always had plenty of time and on rarer occasions had plenty of money, provided a natural market for poets and story-tellers, on whose work they left a clear impression. The quest theme, which became so prominent in the romances, echoes the experiences of those who rode forth to seek adventure and a lady, and some of the troubadours (Marcabru most of all) celebrated the ideal of youth, *iouvens*, as a time of prowess and joy. We must consider later how the writers used these themes, but our immediate purpose is to observe their social origin and significance.

Another group within the nobility with its own special interests was that of the ladies. We must beware of supposing, as is often said, that the status of women was rising in the twelfth century; the process seems to be more subtle and complex than that. The great lady had always enjoyed an important position in society. Tenth-century Germany had been ruled for a time by empresses as regents, and Adela of Blois governed her county for several years. Conversely, Henry II kept his wife, Eleanor of Aquitaine, imprisoned for the last fifteen years of his life, and the cult of courtly love, of which she was a patron, did not save her. What was happening was that the image of the ideal woman was changing around the year 1100. The epics or *chansons de geste* admired the capable wife or mother, who could run their households and protect their estates in the absence of their men, and it is likely that in this they were expressing older and more conservative attitudes. In the newer forms of twelfth-century literature the heroine is young and beautiful. Even ladies of blameless moral reputation welcomed their new role, at least in moderation. The wife of Henry I of England, Matilda, and his sister Adela, both received elegantly flattering verses from leading French humanists, Marbod of Rennes and Baudri of Bourgueil. In less cautious circles, as in the troubadour poetry of the south, the admiration was a great deal more frank. Whatever the literary origin of the new cult of love and beauty, and this is still in dispute, it corresponded to a marked change of social taste and convention. The early twelfth century was a period of experiment in dress. The long hair and effeminate attire of the courts of the period dismayed those of traditional temperament, and on one occasion a preacher succeeded in persuading Henry I and his court to have their hair cut short, then and there. Ladies' dress was changing markedly, especially in France. The old long robes and full head-dress, which covered the hair entirely and concealed the body, were replaced in France by a robe which fitted very tightly down to the waist, where it was flared so as to hang in pleats. On the head a small cap was worn, and the hair allowed to fall (often in two plaits) to the waist. The new style expressed an admiration of youth and beauty which was essentially a new ideal. Social and cultural changes such as this offered to the individual, or rather imposed upon him, decisions about personal preferences and personal values, and the literature of the twelfth century reflects such conflicts, and the hesitation of the individual when faced with them. Many different views, for instance, might be taken of courtly love. Some troubadours saw in love the fulfilment of joy and courtesy (Bernard of Ventadour), others were sceptical about the possibility of true love (Marcabru), and others again saw glory as lying in warfare rather than in love (Bertrand de Born). For some, true love overcame all other values, even that of prowess in battle, and had no connection with the bond of marriage. This was the position taken by Chrétien de Troyes in his story of Lancelot, *The Knight of the Cart*, although he was probably writing under pressure from his patron and perhaps with a partly satirical intent. In most of his works Chrétien took the different view that the proper fulfilment of love lies within marriage. We must consider this in more detail later. For the time being the point is that new social and cultural circumstances were forcing upon the individual choices in important areas of consciousness where previously they had scarcely existed.

A further change took place in yet another area of society, in the creation of a large class of men with an advanced education acquired in the rising cathedral schools and universities. The availability of this group made possible a managerial revolution both in Church and State. The kingdoms of the eleventh century had possessed little by way of a trained civil service, but by 1200 most secular governments commanded the services of skilled lawyers and highly literate clerks, who could be employed in administration, the keeping of records, and diplomacy. By no means all these men had studied in one of the major schools, but many had, and the rest had benefited from the greatly improved level of learning. There is room for doubt whether the unknown author of "Glanvil", the great late-twelfth-century treatise on English law, was a university man, and whether he had received a systematic training in Roman law; but there is no question that his treatise was incomparably more clear and consistent in its planning than the collections of the early twelfth century. A similar development was taking place in the Church, where the advent about the middle of the century of the "officials" provided the bishops with an administration which greatly improved their control of the dioceses, and equipped the papacy with the machinery it needed to centralize more fully the Church in western Europe. All these administrators in the service of the Church, and many of those who worked for secular governments, were clergy, and they were faced by the personal problem that there was no pattern of ethical behaviour to guide and justify their way of life. To men whose whole work lay in helping to run society, a world-renouncing code of the old monastic kind was useless, but neither were they warriors or courtiers in the ordinary sense. That the ethical problem was an acute personal one may be seen in the career of Peter of Blois, who abandoned the service of Henry II to work as an ecclesiastical administrator. He bitterly criticized those who devoted their lives to the courts of kings, but was also acid about the new class of ecclesiastical officials, to which in a sense he belonged personally. The example of Thomas Becket serves to remind us that to waver between the conduct of a courtier and a world-renouncing spirit might not only lead to grave personal distress, but might literally become a matter of life and death. In this situation men sought to formulate a code of conduct for men of business, and some of the classical writings came to them as a revelation. Cicero's *de Officiis*, which is nowadays regarded as uncommonly dull, greatly excited them, for it prescribed a mode of behaviour for people whose work lay in politics or administration, and discussed practical issues for which there was no other guidance available. The new class of intellectuals, however, were not all civil servants, for some of them thought their duty was not to administer, but to criticize and reform. Some of these reformers (for example, John of Salisbury) themselves occupied high administrative office, but others did not. It was characteristic of the humanists, in the twelfth as well as in the sixteenth century, to seek to influence the conduct of government by their criticism and advice. Hildebert of Lavardin was in correspondence with the English court and with several of the great princes of northern France; Aelred of Rievaulx wrote a history of the kings of England in 1153 for the young Henry of Anjou, whom he regarded as the hope of the English; John of Salisbury wrote perhaps the most searching of these criticisms of government, the *Policraticus*, dedicated in 1159 to Becket, who was then royal chancellor; Gerald of Wales in the next generation wrote *The Instruction of a Prince*. As time went on, the divergence between the two groups of intellectuals, the reformers and the civil servants, became more marked, and came to be drawn along educational lines. The demand from governments, whether in Church or State, was increasingly for lawyers, and the classicists and humanists found it difficult to obtain promotion. From this arose the incisive satire against the legal establishment which we shall consider later, and which is highly germane to our subject, because in it the literate individual protests against the dominant values in society.

Twelfth-century society was thus disturbed by the rapid emergence of a whole series of new groups or classes, all of them requiring an ideal on which to model themselves and an ethic to guide them. They thus created a conflict of values, and faced the individual with choices which in the year A.D. 1000 would have been unimaginable. Such men as Abelard or St Bernard had to choose whether to be a knight, a monk, or a secular clerk. If the latter, they had to choose according to their dominant intellectual interest (classics, logic, law, theology) and their hopes for a career (teaching, advancement in Church or State). It was a vigorous, mobile society which generated, like our own age, both optimism and anxiety.

THE FRENCH RENAISSANCE

France dominated the Renaissance of the twelfth century as Italy did that of the fifteenth. Between the two periods there is the further parallel that each country was politically disunited. The power of the Capetian kings was in 1100 effectively limited to a strip of land running from Bourges in the south to Paris in the north. The surrounding French-speaking provinces (Champagne, Burgundy, Blois-Chartres, Anjou, Normandy, Flanders) had a long tradition of independence, and each was ruled by its own duke or count, who was bound by only precarious ties of loyalty to the Crown. Beyond the Loire the power of the Crown was effectively unknown, and most of these southern provinces were culturally distinct from the north, speaking their own language, Languedoc or Provençal. To a remarkable extent the creative cultural developments of the time took place within about 200 miles of Paris, inside the restricted area of "France" proper. Students flocked from other countries to the great cathedral schools here. The Gothic style of architecture was first developed at the churches of Saint-Denis, Chartres, and Sens, and its connections with the region were so strong that it could later be described in Germany as *opus francigenum*, the French style. The new monastic orders took their origins here, notably the Cistercians, whose influence spread throughout Europe from their great houses of Cîteaux and Clairvaux, where Saint Bernard was abbot. Within this area, too, the foundations of European vernacular literature were being laid. The early *chansons de geste* are French in language and spirit, and so are the early romances. The troubadour lyric was brought to fruition about 200 miles from Paris, in Poitou and the Limousin, near the linguistic boundary between French and Languedoc. To speak of a "French Renaissance" is not to make a claim for the peculiar brilliance of Frenchmen at the time, for France (like Italy later)

was able to attract men from other countries, and many of the
ablest thinkers had originally come from further afield. John of
Salisbury was from England, Peter Abelard from Brittany, and
Anselm of Canterbury and Peter Lombard were Italian, but all
had been drawn to France and came to think of it as their home.
Other countries had the lead in particular fields: Italy in Law,
England in History. Yet those developments which most concern
us, the growth of humanism and of an interest in the individual,
were principally French, and when they are found elsewhere
French influence can often be traced. Aelred of Rievaulx was very
much a northern Englishman by inheritance. He was a son of the
last of the hereditary priests of Hexham, and had been a steward
at the Scottish court. He retained throughout his life a devotion
towards the northern saints, and a keen interest in English history.
He once explained that the first Cistercian monastery in England
(at Waverley, in Surrey) was not very influential because it had
been founded "in a corner"—an admirably northern point of
view. Yet his devotion and his theological interests were unmistak-
ably influenced by French ideas. The first settlement at Rievaulx
had come direct from France; he was urged to write his earliest
book by Saint Bernard, who had met him on a visit to Clairvaux
in 1142; and, as we shall see, as a thinker he has to be included
in the "Cistercian" school along with Bernard and William of
Saint Thierry.

The pre-eminence of France in the new thinking rested upon the
rapid development of French society. The changes which were
considered in the last section were more rapid there than elsewhere.
Paris and the Flemish cities represent a rapid change to an urban
civilization; the demand for supplies from the Flemish burghers
gave a golden opportunity to French agriculture, and the new
pattern of lordship developed quickly in the Ile de France. From
all this there arose a strong French nationalism, which we have
already noticed in the self-confidence of the Frankish nobility,
but was not confined to them. In a phrase common to vernacular
poetry and scholarly letters, the land was honoured as "lovely
France", *douce France, dulcis Francia.* Guibert of Nogent called
his history of the First Crusade *Gesta Dei per Francos*, God's
Deeds through the French, and smugly remarked that the title

"is not arrogant, and is a tribute to the honour of the race".[8]
The French were also conscious of a new role as cultural leaders
of Europe. In a famous passage, Chrétien de Troyes wrote
enthusiastically:

> This our books have taught us: that Greece had the first
> renown in chivalry and in learning. Then came chivalry to
> Rome, and the heyday of learning, which is now come into
> France. God grant that she may be maintained there, and that
> her home there please her so much that the honour which has
> come to dwell in France may never depart from her.[9]

Chrétien was here setting out a theme which is to be found several
times in learned circles in France. Interestingly enough, the idea
of the transfer of learning, *translatio studii*, from east to west
had originated among the scholars of the Carolingian revival.
It reappeared among writers excited by the growth of scholarship
in France during the twelfth century.* This expansion was all
the more exciting for being sudden. Guibert of Nogent commented
on the difficulty of finding teachers in his childhood (he was born
in 1053) as compared with their abundance when he wrote his
autobiography about 1115:

> A little before that time, and still partly in my own time, there
> was a great shortage of teachers of grammar. Almost none of
> them could be found in towns, and few enough in cities; and
> those who could be found were slender in knowledge, and were
> not even comparable with the wandering scholars of our own
> day.[10]

Guibert's impression of rapid development was apparently correct.
There can indeed be no renaissance without a preparation, and
the rise of the French cathedral schools can probably be traced
back to Fulbert, first the chancellor and then the bishop of Chartres

* The fullest and most interesting exposition of the theme is in fact in
a German writer, Otto of Freising, who is often regarded as the most
important influence in disseminating it in the west. However, A. G.
Jongkees has argued persuasively that it was primarily a French idea,
suggested to Otto during his studies at Paris. See his article, "Translatio
Studii", in *Miscellanea Mediaevalia in Memoriam Jan Frederik Niermeyer*
(Groningen 1967), pp. 41–51.

(1006–28). Fulbert was an outstanding teacher, who left behind him a group of eminent and enthusiastic pupils. Nevertheless, it is still correct to stress the speed of progress between 1070 and 1100, particularly in the prevailing standard of Latinity. There are not many signs of the writing of prose and poetry of high quality in the years before 1070, but by 1100 the ability was widespread. Hildebert of Lavardin, Marbod of Rennes, and Anselm of Canterbury were all writing elegant Latin, the first two of them in a style close to that of some of the classics; and in the next generation this skill spread even more widely. It was an age of rapid development in literature and learning.

THE RETURN TO THE PAST

Perhaps no vital and progressive society has ever had so rich a sense of its inheritance, and such a humility in face of the achievements of the past, as this one. The spirit of the humanists is nobly expressed in Hildebert's great poem on the ruins of Rome:

> The city now is fallen; I can find
> No worthier epitaph than: "This was Rome".
> Yet not the flight of years, nor flame nor sword
> Could fully wipe away its loveliness . . .
> Bring wealth, new marble and the help of gods,
> Let craftsmen's hands be active in the work—
> Yet shall these standing walls no equal find,
> Nor can these ruins even be restored.
> The care of men once built so great a Rome,
> The care of gods could not dissolve its stones.
> Divinities admire their faces carved,
> And wish themselves the equal of those forms.
> Nature could not make gods as fair of face
> As man created images of Gods.

> urbs cecidit, de qua si quicquam dicere dignum
>   moliar, hoc potero dicere "Roma fuit".
> non tamen annorum series, non flamma nec ensis
>   ad plenum potuit hoc abolere decus . . .

confer opes marmorque novum superumque favorem,
   artificum vigilent in nova facta manus,
non tamen aut fieri par stanti machina muro,
   aut restaurari sola ruina potest.
cura hominum potuit tantam componere Romam,
   quantam non potuit solvere cura deum.
hic superum formas superi mirantur et ipsi,
   et cupiunt fictis vultibus esse pares.
non potuit Natura deos hoc ore creare,
   quo miranda deum signa creavit homo.[11]

It would, however, be quite wrong to suppose that the twelfth-century Renaissance consisted solely, or even mainly, of a re-birth of classical knowledge. With a remarkable unanimity, men turned to the records of the past to discover the meaning of the present: to the classics, the Bible, the Fathers, the Roman Law, and the Canon Law; to the Rule of Saint Benedict and to the desert Fathers. People even made private and individual forays into the past to discover the history and the patron saints of their churches. Abbot Suger of Saint-Denis was deeply attached to the writings of pseudo-Dionysius, which influenced his approach to architecture and the arts, and hence the rebuilding of the abbey church, an event crucial in the emergence of Gothic architecture.[12] His interest had undoubtedly been aroused by the belief, resting on a triple confusion of names, that the author was the patron saint of his abbey. (During his short stay as a monk at Saint-Denis after 1118, Abelard, with his unfailing talent for getting himself into trouble, had unravelled at least part of this knot of false identifications, but his researches were neither believed nor welcomed by the brethren.) Similarly, Gilbert de la Porrée, bishop of Poitiers, studied the works of Hilary, his saintly predecessor, and absorbed his views on trinitarian theology. This led to a great deal of difficulty, for Hilary had learned his theology in the east, and his teaching on the Trinity was very different in expression, and perhaps also in content, from the ideas which the west was to receive from Saint Augustine.

In this massive recovery of the past we may discern two purposes. The first was technical, the acquisition of information.

Roman Law obviously turned on the use of ancient material; so did medicine, and the developing scientific studies; so did logic, which still rested mainly on the use of those works of Aristotle which Boethius had made available. With studies of this kind we shall not be much concerned in this book, for they contributed little to the discovery of the individual, but it is important to remember that they played a large part in the total body of study and relied on knowledge from the classical past. The second motive is more important for our purposes, and less easy to define. It was a search for new attitudes, ideals, and elegances. Men realized the inadequacy of the immediate past, and, as many reformers do, they turned to distant and more civilized ages to repair the inadequacy of their immediate inheritance. What they found depended on what they were looking for, and their requirements were varied. The appearance of a city civilization, and of a more sophisticated aristocracy, had once more the same effect as it had in antiquity. It drove some men into world-renunciation, and in others it created respect for the individual and confidence in humanity. Both groups were naturally drawn to their great predecessors, who had stated their views lucidly in a former age. The Cistercians may be taken as the prime examples of world-renunciation. Their appeal was to the Rule of Saint Benedict, interpreted in the strictest and most rigorous sense, and to the example of the desert Fathers. Representatives of this world-renouncing group would be less inclined to use the pagan classics, although on occasions they did so. Over against them one must place the world-affirmers, who valued the classics, in part at least, because they provided an ethic, or an elegant way of life, for a man in the world. To this group belongs Abelard, with his confidence in the power of human reason; John of Salisbury, with his attempt to provide guidance for statesmen; and the many writers who drew on Cicero's *de Officiis* and on Seneca because they contained the material for what we would call a secular ethic. Although this great division into two groups contains some truth, it is much too crude for the historical facts. As we shall see in later chapters, one of the fascinating features of this period is the combination in each school of writers of renunciation and affirmation. The Cistercians undoubtedly felt violent hostility to the secular world; Saint Bernard disciplined his body with ferocious self-denial, and quite often wrote as if the monastic way was the only secure road to salvation. Yet we shall find later that Bernard was greatly concerned with personal sincerity and motivation, and that for him the spiritual life was a way of self-discovery which preserved the dignity and integrity of the individual even in the moment of union with God. Similarly, the finest treatise on friendship in the period was written by the Cistercian Aelred of Rievaulx, and was based consciously on Cicero's *de Amicitia*. Conversely, John of Salisbury and Abelard both appear much less confident about human society when we remember that they had no idea of Cicero as a politician and that their ideal of a philosopher was an ascetic who had withdrawn from the world.[13] The satirists, too, combined a brilliant literary style and piercing wit with a world-despair and expectation of the coming of Antichrist worthy of the most extreme ascetic. No simple formula will cover the motives of men at this time, for they combined confidence and despair in ways which were subtle, and sometimes self-contradictory.

As a result of this mixture of motives, men were unquestionably influenced by the classics, but in turn the classical writers themselves suffered a sea-change. It has been wisely said that while one may speak of a twelfth-century Humanism, it can in no sense be regarded as a true Classicism.[14] The reasons for this situation were manifold. Although the twelfth century was passionately interested in history, it had not developed a critical historical sense; indeed, this did not begin to appear until the eighteenth century. There was no conception of the difference between Roman society and the contemporary world. As Shakespeare dressed his Roman statesmen in doublet and hose, so the romances of the twelfth century peopled Greece, Troy, and ancient Britain with knights and their ladies, and Barbarossa thought himself to be unambiguously one of the Roman emperors. This lack of historical sense was complicated by the fact that, outside the ranks of the really outstanding scholars, few classical works were read as a whole. They were known in *florilegia* or collections of quotations, which frequently were ascribed to the wrong author, and usually included the passages most susceptible to interpretation or misinterpretation in a Christian sense. We must insist, moreover, that the men of the time did not usually *expect* to discern any great difference between Christian and pagan philosophy. As we saw in an earlier chapter, the Church in the patristic period had absorbed a good deal of classical thought, which could be found embodied in Ambrose, Augustine, and Boethius. It would be as correct to think of one Christian-classical inheritance as of two distinct traditions. The poets proved more disturbing to the twelfth century than the classical prose-writers, for it was much less easy to fragment poetry into *florilegia* or to digest it into theological systems. Lucan, Virgil, and Ovid continued to provide unassimilated statements of non-Christian beliefs that perpetually challenged medieval ingenuity in disposing of unwelcome ideas.

The system of education itself tended to obscure the fact that the classical world offered ideas which differed considerably from twelfth-century attitudes. The foundation course was provided by the seven liberal arts, and of these the most basic was Grammar. This term (like "mathematics" nowadays) covered an enormous range of attainment, from the schoolboy painfully construing a simple text to the finest flower of humanist scholarship. It appears that the lectures of Bernard of Chartres, the famous Grammar teacher of about 1100, began with comments upon the construction and usages in a particular text, and then proceeded to the discussion of the moral and philosophical teaching given there. The result was that both ethics and philosophy could be studied as a branch of Grammar. At its best this literary approach meant that the student came face to face with both the style and the thought of a given writer, and there were some outstanding successes of this kind. The use made of Cicero's *de Amicitia* (which proved particularly to the taste of the period), and of Ciceronian ideas in John of Salisbury's *Policraticus*, are genuine examples of new vision introduced from a past age. Inevitably, many of the consequences of this mode of teaching were less satisfactory. As in the sixteenth century, much humanist writing stayed at the level of stylistic imitation. Serlo of Wilton wrote verse of spectacular obscenity in the Ovidian manner, but it seems likely that what interested him was style and not pornographic content.[15] Even when the thought of a writer had genuinely been absorbed along with the style, there was a temptation to put it on and take it off like a suit of clothes according to the occasion. When in 1120 the young William, heir to Henry I of England, was lost in the "White Ship", Hildebert wrote to his father a letter of consolation couched in terms of which Seneca would have been proud. It is entirely Stoic, encouraging the king to bear, in face of adversity, an unchanged countenance. It is interesting to see that Hildebert was less impassive in face of his own misfortunes, for his earlier exile to England had produced some highly passionate letters about sharing the sufferings of Christ. Between Hildebert the humanist and Hildebert the Christian there is in fact a chasm. One can find bridges across it, but no solid ground.

We find, therefore, an extreme variety of approach to classical writers. The poets were Christianized with great vigour. Virgil was honoured with elaborate allegorical interpretations, designed, it was said, "to find some gold in the mass of mud".[16] The treatment of Ovid, a great favourite of the age, was more diverse and interesting. We have already seen that Serlo of Wilton regarded him as an excellent stylist for technical imitation. Other writers found in him a quarry for that favourite theme of the age, the discussion of love, and they were delighted with the range of attitudes which were expressed in his works. In this sense he must certainly be regarded as an important source for the love-literature of the time, and it is interesting to find that Chrétien de Troyes' first works were adaptations of Ovid. Yet others found in him an expression of the soul's love for its creator, handling him as the Song of Songs had been used long before. His most surprising appearance is as a stalwart defender of chastity, a version of his approach to life which would have perplexed the poet himself. The range of attitudes to Ovid exemplifies the contemporary approach to the classics. It had the grave disadvantage that there was little awareness of an encounter with a different society and with philosophies of a non-Christian kind. It possessed, however, the merits of its defects. Since contemporaries were scarcely aware of classical writers as a phenomenon foreign to themselves, they were able to absorb easily those parts of their message which were appropriate to the new needs. It was not felt unsuitable to use the Delphic "know thyself" as a basis for a new self-awareness, because they did not see the classics as alien to twelfth-century circumstances.

Their attitude has been well summed up by Dom Jean Leclercq:

> It also made possible an amazing contact with ancient literature. The vital use they made of it is something that we can no longer achieve in our times. Ovid, Virgil and Horace *belonged* to these men as personal property; they were not an alien possession to which to refer and quote with reverence—and with bibliographical references. Medieval men claimed for themselves the right to make the authors conform to usage, to the actual needs of a living culture. Each of these authors was quoted freely and from memory and even without acknowledgement. The important thing was not what he had said or meant . . . but what a Christian of the tenth or twelfth century could find in him.[17]

THE PROBLEM OF AUTHORITY

So far, the emphasis has been placed upon the unity which existed, in twelfth-century eyes, between the Christian and classical inheritance. Patristic writers had already incorporated classical ideas, and this encouraged the interpretation of classical writers in Christian terms. At one point, however, a distinction must be made. If great respect was shown in many circles to the authors of the classical past, the authority of early Christian writing— of the Scriptures and the Fathers—was still greater and more unquestionable. A primitive society has few sources of knowledge except the wisdom of the elders, and even the more sophisticated society which was now evolving was aware of the great amount which it owed to the learning of the past. The famous remark that they were like dwarfs sitting on the backs of giants delicately expressed their combination of self-confidence and respect for the past.*

The rapid growth of learning, however, soon posed an acute problem of authority. The return to the formative documents of the Christian past, and their more intense and careful study, led to a series of discoveries which were greeted with either excitement

* On the restricted and specific meaning of this simile, see, however, E. Jeauneau, "Nains et Géants", *Entretiens sur la Renaissance du 12ᵉ siècle*, pp. 21–38.

or dismay. A serious reading of the Rule of Saint Benedict revealed that the monasteries of Europe were not living according to the regulations which they had sworn to obey—an undeniable fact which was eagerly used by reformers to trouble the conscience of conservatives, and which provided new orders such as the Cistercians with a clear programme: "Back to the Rule". A careful examination of canon law indicated that the Church in 1050 was far from observing the decrees which were supposed to govern its life, and this realization provided one of the main motives of the papal reform movement. The reading of the Fathers in the light of the better knowledge of logic revealed that the Augustinian doctrine of the Trinity, for example, was immensely more complex and sophisticated than the simple creeds which had been accepted as adequate in the immediate past, and that it raised a variety of issues which required consideration. It was therefore discovered that the existing practice and belief in monasticism, in canon law, and in doctrine, was in serious disaccord with the authoritative standards of the past, and this inevitably confronted individuals with a series of choices which they found difficult and painful. The situation was in many ways like the reassessment of the doctrine, liturgy, and discipline of the Church which is currently in progress, and it was quite as painful for the men of the time.

The return to a fuller study of canon law and the Fathers led to a second discovery. Not surprisingly, these ancient authorities were found not to be speaking directly to the circumstances of the twelfth century, and it was necessary for men to take the initiative in solving problems for which they were given no real guidance in their texts. For example, although there was a considerable body of teaching about marriage in the Fathers and the canon law, the issues raised within Roman society were quite different from those facing the Church of 1100, confronted by the customs of Germanic nations, and the later marriage law of the Western Church was essentially a creation of the twelfth century. The sacramental theology of the Fathers was closely related to the experience of community within the Church, and was not readily comprehensible to a generation which lived in a world where every man was officially born as a Christian. In consequence, the doctrine of the sacraments was entirely rethought, and the ideas which were subsequently to be regarded as official Catholic teaching (the seven sacraments and transubstantiation, for example) were formulated in the twelfth century. In the same way the thinkers of the new age found older theories of the atonement inadequate, and produced their own alternatives, which expressed more vividly, as did those of Anselm and Abelard, the part of Christ's human suffering and the individual relationship between the sinner and Christ.* In view of the inclination which one sometimes finds to regard the medieval Church as *semper eadem*, too faithful or too timid to change its doctrine, it is important to stress this creativity, and the courageous thinking of individuals which made it possible. The doctrine and discipline of the Western Church was modified to meet a new situation (new, that is, against the context in which the Fathers wrote and in which the older principles of canon law had been formulated) presented by the fact that Church and society were now identical in membership. The significance of this new situation was pointed out by Otto of Freising in his book *The Two Cities*:

> I seem to myself to have composed a history not of two cities but virtually of one only, which I call the Church. For although the elect and reprobate are in one household, yet I cannot call those cities two as I did above; I must call them properly but one.[18]

The return to the Fathers thus produced two types of issues for the men of the twelfth-century Renaissance: it confronted them directly with a challenge to renew the life and thinking of the patristic Church, and indirectly with a challenge to produce new

* There is something of a mystery why the twelfth century saw such a new start in atonement theology. It was for a long time supposed that the Fathers had no atonement doctrine; Gustav Aulén went far to correct this view in his stimulating book *Christus Victor*, but without fully explaining the radical break with the past which took place about 1100. The explanation may be that the best thought on the subject was that of Greek Fathers unknown to Anselm and Abelard. Latin tradition was decidedly weak on this point, and, as we shall see in subsequent chapters, the theory of the atonement raises issues crucial to twelfth-century thought about the individual.

solutions where the old ones were no longer applicable. The third problem which it produced was, to them, the most burning of all: the discovery that the revered authorities disagreed with one another. Peter Abelard wrote a masterly analysis of this problem in the preface to his *Sic et Non*, explaining that

> within so great a volume of material, some of the opinions of even the saints appear, not only to differ from one another, but actually to be in conflict.[19]

The problem was acute. The previous centuries of the Church's history had enthroned authority upon a pedestal, and it was not easy to take the view that some of the Fathers had merely been wrong. Moreover, the poverty of historical techniques was such that men could not see how different the situation now was, and how canons, or expositions of Christian experience, from the fourth century could not be applied without revision to the Church of the early twelfth. For the solution of these problems of authority they turned to the developing techniques of logic or dialectic, from which it was hoped for two sorts of help. One was the reconciliation of conflicting authorities, according to rules skilfully propounded by Abelard in the *Sic et Non*. It was hoped that, when considerations of different terminology, intention, and situation had been sifted, and all distinctions made, the area of irreducible disagreement would be left as a very small one. This seems to us a rashly optimistic assumption, but in the context of the age it was an understandable, and indeed necessary, line of investigation. It was, moreover, accompanied by a far more radical approach: the subjection of traditional doctrine to criticism on rational criteria. This was an important manifestation of the individualism of the age, and must therefore command our attention for a short time.

In a society so monolithic in belief it must be recognized that human reason was regarded as offering far fewer options than it would today. Christianity was almost the only organized world-view with which Europeans were familiar. Islam provided no alternative, if only because in the early twelfth century it was thought to consist of superstitions so bizarre that no one (least of all the Moslem) could conceivably believe them. In spite of the growing knowledge of the classics, only a tiny handful of scholars was able to form a genuine picture of one of the classical schools of thought, or to appreciate the arguments which might be derived from it against the faith of the Church. In these circumstances a view looked rational only if it were already close to Christianity, and it was an achievement to have formulated the idea of rational criticism at all. One source of the idea was the Jews, whose well-articulated reasons for denying the gospel were familiar to many theologians. Perhaps more important were the questions which occurred to intelligent men within the Church, for it must be remembered that people did not come to Christianity out of prior conviction; they *started* as Christians, and then found that they were troubled by doubts or questions. Such doubts were not at all unusual, and the natural place to look for an answer was reason or philosophy—as with King Amaury of Jerusalem who asked Archbishop William of Tyre for the philosophical arguments for a future life, which might be advanced to persuade any one who was not convinced by the teaching of the Scriptures.[20] The investigation of the rational basis of Christian belief was certainly not confined to thinkers who were regarded as heretical, or at least questionable. In many ways St Anselm of Canterbury was the most active champion of this attempt. In a series of works published at the end of the eleventh century he attempted to find a secure rational basis for belief in the existence of God (the "ontological" proof) and to demonstrate the logical necessity of the incarnation:

> Leaving out Christ, as if he had never been heard of, the book will prove by necessary reasons that without him no man could ever be saved.[21]

Such a rational approach, whatever its limitations, involved its advocates in a good deal of independent judgement. Writers of exemplary orthodoxy were on occasion willing to back their own judgement against the teaching of tradition. St Anselm cavalierly swept out of his way a view which rested on a great deal of patristic support:

> As to that which we are accustomed to say, that God was obliged to act against the devil to liberate man rather by justice than by

power; and that when the devil killed him in whom was no cause of death, and who was God, he justly lost the power he had over sinners; . . . I do not see what force it has.[22]

In this matter of reason and authority there were sharp divisions between conservatives and liberals. When, just before 1140, Abelard incautiously advertised his disagreement with the Fathers, he was scathingly attacked by St Bernard:

> "It must be recognized" (he says) "that all our doctors since the Apostles have agreed on this: that the devil had dominion and power over man, and possessed him by right, because man consented willingly to the devil by his own free choice . . . But it seems to us" (says he) "that the devil never had any right over man, except in so far as God allowed it as a jailer; nor did the Son of God take flesh to liberate man." Which shall I call the more intolerable in these words—the blasphemy or the arrogance? Which the more damnable—the rashness or the impiety? . . . Does he not deservedly provoke every man's hand against him, whose hand is against every man? "All", he says, "think thus; but *I* do not think so." And who may *you* be? What have you to give that is better? What have you found that is deeper? What special secret do you say has been revealed to you, since you so surpass the saints and overbear the sages?[23]

The clash between Bernard and Abelard raised openly the question of individual judgement in matters of faith, but on the whole it is striking that this issue did not present itself in the twelfth century in anything like the acute form which it took in the sixteenth and seventeenth. Great changes were introduced into the life and thought of the Church with only a minimal conflict between the individual and the hierarchy. For this remarkable fact we may adduce two reasons. One is that the papacy itself was in many ways a champion of change. Gregory VII did not hesitate to employ lay power, and even popular risings, to enforce reform upon local churches; Alexander III and Innocent III both contributed personally to the major alteration of the Church's marriage discipline; and the papacy was sympathetic to the work of the cathedral schools and universities, Abelard himself having considerable support within the Roman curia. The other explanation is that, as we have already seen, the age believed that the objective use of reason would lead men to, or at least towards, the acceptance of the Christian faith. This was the assumption on which Anselm's whole philosophy rested, and Bernard himself had no objection to the use of reason in religious matters, for he wrote letters of personal recommendation on behalf of two of its leading exponents, the humanist John of Salisbury and the theologian Peter Lombard. While there was naturally a variety of views on this question, even the most reactionary thinkers were inclined to welcome the use of reason for the reconciliation of discordant authorities, and to object only when it was applied in the factious pursuit of personal glory or in the explanation of the being of God, which was beyond rational analysis. Bernard believed, rightly or wrongly, that both these faults were evident in Abelard, and it was this conviction, rather than any hostility to a rational approach as such, which led to his attempt to silence him.

The problems raised by the use of patristic authority therefore gave scope for creative thinking, but it produced only to a slight extent a direct confrontation between tradition and individual opinion. The new ferment in theology contributed to the discovery of the individual, but we shall find this manifested more obviously in other parts of the cultural scene.

4 The Search for the Self

The Answer of the Delphic Apollo was famous among the Greeks: "Man, know yourself". The same thing was said by Solomon, or rather Christ in the Song of Songs: "If you do not know yourself, go forth".
WILLIAM OF SAINT THIERRY, *The Nature of Body and Soul*, prologue,[1] *c.* 1130–40

Ethics: or, Know yourself
TITLE OF BOOK BY PETER ABELARD, *c.* 1135

Who is more contemptible than he who scorns a knowledge of himself?
JOHN OF SALISBURY, *Policraticus*,[2] 1159

The word "individual" did not, in the twelfth century, have the same meaning as it does today. The nearest equivalents were *individuum, individualis*, and *singularis*, but these terms belonged to logic rather than to human relations. They do, nevertheless, demand our brief attention, for logic is closer to life than we often suppose, and the categories a man uses are those which he finds appropriate to his experience. A central problem of medieval philosophy was the relation of the individual object (*unum singulare*) with the general or universal class to which it belonged, and humanity was often taken as a test case in this argument. A correlation can frequently be observed between a thinker's concept of the universal and his assumptions about man; indeed, if it were not so, it would constitute a serious rift in the whole fabric of his thought, although it would be unwise to assume that the formal logic was connected in a simple and direct way with the view of man. It is interesting to find that Anselm of Canterbury, whose atonement theology turned on the assumption of the solidarity of mankind, believed strongly in the reality of universals: "If someone does not understand how several men are in species but a single man, how can he understand that . . . several persons can be one God, yet each a perfect God?"[3]

Conversely, Abelard stood much closer to modern individualism, both in his idea of salvation and in his rejection of general concepts: "Although people say that Socrates and Plato are one in their humanity, how can that be accepted, when it is obvious that all men are different from each other both in matter and in form?"[4] Abelard is an interesting case in point, for he was anxious as his argument proceeded to avoid the obvious conclusion from this extreme individualism in logic, and to assign some partial reality to universals. It is therefore at least plausible to suggest that his starting-point was his actual experience of men (whom he personally regarded as very distinct individuals) and that this experience imposed itself upon his logic.

Whatever we think of this somewhat speculative connection between logic and life, there is no doubt that the concept of an "individual", in so far as it existed, belonged to the former and not to the latter. The age had, however, other words to express its interest in personality. We hear a great deal of "the self", not expressed indeed in that abstract way, but in such terms as "knowing oneself", "descending into oneself", or "considering oneself". Another common term was *anima*, which was used, ambiguously in our eyes, for both the spiritual identity ("soul") of a man and his directing intelligence ("mind"). Yet another was "the inner man", a phrase found in Otloh of Saint Emmeram and Guibert of Nogent, who spoke also of the "inner mystery".[5] Their vocabulary, while it was not the same as ours, was therefore rich in terms suited to express the ideas of self-discovery and self-exploration.

"KNOW YOURSELF"

Self-knowledge was one of the dominant themes of the age. Two texts usually came to mind, those which appear in the passage from William of Saint Thierry which stands at the head of this chapter: Song of Songs 1.7 and the Delphic "Know yourself". This command had long been accepted within the tradition of the

Church, and in the eyes of the twelfth century Augustine was the master of the art of self-knowledge:[6]

> For now, while [the soul] is still in the body, it is said to her, "Where is your God?" But her God is within, He is spiritually within and spiritually beyond: . . . the soul cannot succeed in finding Him, except by passing through herself.

This idea of self-knowledge as the path to God was taken up particularly by writers in the monastic or eremitical tradition, such as Peter Damiani and the Cistercians. Among the talented men in this group Bernard, abbot of Clairvaux from 1115 to 1153, was the most famous, and perhaps the most penetrating thinker. Other Cistercians were more systematic in their treatment of the theme of self-knowledge. William of Saint Thierry was a native of Liége who entered the Benedictine house of Saint Thierry at Rheims. He soon fell under Bernard's influence, and wanted to become a Cistercian, eventually, in spite of Bernard's dissuasion, entering the newly founded Cistercian house at Signy in 1153. Also under Bernard's influence was the attractive and able Englishman Aelred, whom we have already met in a previous chapter, and who was abbot of the Cistercian house of Rievaulx from 1147 to 1167. These writers all insisted on self-knowledge as fundamental. Thus Bernard wrote to Pope Eugenius, a fellow-Cistercian, about 1150: "Begin by considering yourself—no, rather, end by that. . . . For you, you are the first; you are also the last."[7] So did Aelred of Rievaulx: "How much does a man know, if he does not know himself?"[8] The Cistercian school was not the only one to attach such a value to self-knowledge. About 1108 Guibert of Nogent began his history of the Crusade with a modern-sounding reflection about the difficulty of determining motive:

> It is hardly surprising if we make mistakes in narrating the actions of other people, when we cannot express in words even our own thoughts and deeds; in fact, we can hardly sort them out in our own minds. It is useless to talk about intentions, which, as we know, are often so concealed as scarcely to be discernible to the understanding of the inner man.[9]

Self-knowledge, then, was a generally popular ideal.

Equally widespread was the desire for self-expression. We hear the authentic voice of the individual, speaking of his own desires and experiences. One field in which this now became apparent was the sermon. The period 1050–1200 saw a huge increase both in the preaching and in the preservation of sermons. As we would expect, the general spirit of these works is an objective one: the preacher's task was to expound, not himself, but the word of God and the doctrine of the Church. One school of preachers, however, was much inclined to stress the value of their own experience in the interpretation to others of the gospel. Guibert of Nogent regarded the promotion of self-understanding as the main function of the preacher, and thought that this had to come from the preacher's own self-analysis:

> No preaching seems to me more profitable than that which reveals a man to himself, and replaces in his inner self, that is in his mind, what has been projected outside; and which convincingly places him, as in a portrait [*quodammodo depictum*], before his own eyes. . . . Whoever has the duty of teaching, if he wishes to be perfectly equipped, can first learn in himself, and afterwards profitably teach to others, what the experience of his inner struggles has taught, which is much more abundant than we can express, according to the way the successes and failures which he has experienced have impressed themselves on his memory.[10]

Saint Bernard was outstanding among preachers of this type, drawing freely upon his own spiritual experience, and on at least one occasion, his sermon on the death of his brother Gerard, the exposition of the Scriptures was driven out of his mind almost completely by the cry of his own personal pain:

> It is said to me, "Do not feel any pain". But I do feel pain, and that in spite of myself; I have not the insensibility of a stone, nor is my flesh of bronze; I have feeling assuredly, and sharp pain . . . Someone has called this carnal; I do not deny that it is human, just as I do not deny that I am a man. If that does not suffice, then I shall not deny that it is carnal.[11]

Another form in which the individual declared his wants and needs was lyric poetry. Latin verse had never been written so well since the golden age of Roman literature, and poets had a wide range of metres at their command. They could, and did, write in classical style, but after centuries of long, and often painful, experiment a type of verse had at last been developed which employed accentual metres and rhyme schemes. This form was close to the vernacular, and enabled a poet to speak his mind with directness and simplicity. Many of these lyrics were designed as songs, or were influenced by songs, and one of their prime objectives was the sincere and immediate expression of emotion. The desire of the individual had not, since classical days, received such a clear statement:

The trembling balance of the mind	*In trutina mentis dubia*
Is easily to opposites inclined,	*fluctuant contraria,*
Love's lechery and modest chastity.	*lascivus amor et pudicitia.*

But I will choose what I see now,	*Sed eligo, quod video:*
And so my neck I gladly bow	*collum iugo prebeo,*
To take that most sweet yoke on me.	*ad iugum tamen suave transeo.*[12]

The balanced, general reflection of the first stanza suddenly explodes in the second into a passionate choice, with four first-person verbs in three short lines. This concern to express personal emotion is apparent also in the way biblical characters were sometimes regarded. Abelard wrote a series of magnificent *Laments* or *Planctus* which he put into the mouths of people from the Old Testament, whom he saw, not as forerunners of Christ, but as real individuals in a tragic situation—Dinah lamenting the slaughter which she had innocently occasioned, Jacob mourning his missing sons.* A passage which appealed to more than one poet was the lament of David over Jonathan, for this provided the opportunity for that favourite topic of the age, the loss of a friend. This was finely handled by an English writer popular at the time, Lawrence of Durham:

* See the views of Peter Dronke, *Poetic Individuality*, ch. 4: "One aspect of Samson had never been seen till Abelard saw it: Samson as a man who suffered, a failure, a tragic human being" (p. 132).

What shall I do,
Deprived of such a friend, alone?
There never shall be afterward his like,
Nor was there such before. He was my strength,
My rest and my consoling joy. Dear friend,
Part of my soul, I feel my very self
Most bitterly divided in your death.

Quid, inquit, agam?
Heu quid tristis agam, tali priuatus amico?
  Qualis, ut ipse reor, postmodo nullus erit;
Ut firmare queo, nullus fuit. Ipse iuuamen,
  Ipse michi requies, ipse leuamen erat.
Dulcis amans, anime pars magna mee, peramarum
Sensi discidium, te moriente, mei.[13]

At this point, it is necessary to make a distinction. The poetry
we have been considering is personal verse, but not autobiographical. The poet is striving to express a common human experience, and is doing so by putting himself in the position of the
person who suffers or desires. So direct an assertion of personal
feeling was new, at least as far as surviving Latin verse takes us,
and it reminds us how closely allied humanism can be to the
discovery of the individual. Their understanding of the human
condition is made manifest by their ability to declare the emotions
of the individual. Indeed, the author of *In trutina mentis dubia*
creates an almost formal connection between the two, by setting
out in one stanza first a common dilemma and then a cry of
personal desire. The reality of this achievement is not impaired
either by the careful literary construction of the poems (Lawrence
of Durham certainly intended his readers to catch the echoes of
Horace) or by the fact that the author is not speaking of his own
experience. Indeed, on closer examination the distinction between
personal and autobiographical verse proves a difficult one to make.
Lawrence put his lamentation into the mouth of King David, but
we know that he was keenly concerned about friendship and
personally owned a copy of Cicero's *de Amicitia*. It is therefore no
coincidence that David and Jonathan provided the occasion for

some of his finest lines. Similarly, it has been suggested with plausibility that Abelard's own tragic career deepened and enriched the *Laments* which he wrote in the person of biblical figures. Conversely, there is some twelfth-century verse which is openly autobiographical, particularly the work of the egregious Archpoet, to whom we shall return in a later chapter. One is tempted to think, however, that the Archpoet, perhaps consciously, has created a literary *persona* for himself; to entertain his audience he enacts the role of mocker, rake, and blasphemer. It is therefore wise not to concern ourselves too much with the amount of private experience which lies behind the lyrics of the time, and to content ourselves with observing how directly they express the thought of the individual, whose voice had not been heard so clearly for many centuries.

To express a man's feelings in face of life's sorrows and joys was a major concern of the age. We must now consider the manifestations of this in a variety of fields: in church discipline, in psychology, in the writing of autobiographies, and in portraiture.

CONFESSION

The system of discipline which had prevailed in the Church before 1050 appeared, to an age with a new self-awareness, to be in urgent need of reform. Originally the disciplinary arrangements of the Church had been designed to suit a small community. Those who sinned against God and the brotherhood had to be forgiven in the assembly of the Church, after, in the case of serious offences, undergoing a period of exclusion from full membership. This practice was clearly not suitable for the rough Germanic society which succeeded the Roman Empire, and in the Dark Ages the system of discipline had become strangely external, the punishment of an offence by a specific penance. The character of the system may be seen in the penalties imposed on the army of William the Conqueror after the Battle of Hastings in 1066. Nowhere does the document mention inner repentance, and since the supposed penitents were soldiers, it was very probable that they would repeat the offences; a likelihood which apparently did not trouble the authors of the document:

Anyone who knows that he killed a man in the great battle must do penance for one year for each man that he killed. Anyone who wounded a man, and does not know whether he killed him or not, must do penance for forty days for each man he thus struck (if he can remember the number), either continuously or at intervals. Anyone who does not know the number of those he wounded or killed must, at the discretion of his bishop, do penance for one day in each week for the remainder of his life; or, if he can, let him redeem his sin by a perpetual alms, either by building or by endowing a church.[14]

A similar spirit appears in the penance in the *Song of Roland*:

The French dismount and kneel upon the ground,
And the archbishop blesses them from God
And for their penance, orders them to fight.[15]

Such attitudes persisted into the twelfth century and afterwards, but they were being challenged by a new emphasis upon self-examination. A sense of personal sin and unworthiness had always been part of Christian tradition, and it may be found in the piety of the Cluniacs and, in a very exaggerated form, among the Italian hermits. From the early eleventh century onwards penitential hymns in the first person, which had been uncommon earlier, began to be composed, especially for the feast of Saint Mary Magdalene, which became increasingly popular. Associated with this was an awareness that external penance was distinct from inner repentance, and that it was the latter which God valued. About 1047 the south German monk Otloh of Saint Emmeram, trained in a reformed Cluniac tradition, acknowledged that repentance must go deeper than a ceremony: "Although I had then done penance in the abbot's presence, yet, because I had failed to do it before God, against whom alone I had greatly sinned, after a few days I fell into a sickness."[16] The distinction which Otloh made had become so clear to Peter Abelard, nearly a century later, that in one of his hymns on the feast of Mary Magdalene he made a direct attack on the system of public penance, and indeed on any outward observance as distinct from sorrow of heart:

Penitents'	*Paenitentum*
severe correction,	*severa correptio*
when they pay	*Et eorum*
long satisfaction,	*longa satisfactio*
tames the flesh,	*Crebris carnem*
With their frequent fasts	*edomant ieiuniis*
and with their	*Asperisque*
hair-shirts' cruel rasps.	*cruciant ciliciis*
Those expelled	*Et eiectos*
from the church will know	*ab ecclesia*
what it is	*Cunfundit*
shame to undergo.	*erubescentia.*
But the saint	*In hac nihil*
did not suffer thus,	*actum est hoc ordine*
finding God	*Mitiorem*
gentler far than us,	*sensit Deum homine,*
for the Judge	*Rex et iudex*
uses equity,	*idem legem temperat*
nor does God	*Nec attendit,*
who all hearts can see,	*qui cor vere iudicat,*
value more	*Tam temporis*
A long-lasting sentence	*longitudinem*
than a true	*Quam doloris*
sorrowful repentance.	*magnitudinem.*[17]

By this time, indeed, penitential hymns had become so common that Abelard felt obliged to protest, not merely against external penances, but also against compositions whose wording was so emotional as to be insincere:

> There are in fact very few people who, with tears and groans, burning in contemplation or penitent for their sins, can appropriately sing this sort of thing:
>
> > "Sighing we make our prayer;
> > Pardon, O Lord, our sins", or
>
> > "Receive with kindness, Lord,
> > Our weeping and our song."
>
> These are all right for the elect—and therefore only for the minority.[18]

What Abelard wanted, therefore, was neither external acts nor emotional gush, but true inner sorrow for sin.

This was a matter on which Abelard himself felt particularly strongly, but in essence he was expressing, in his usual incisive way, the convictions of most of his contemporaries. The result of this stress upon inward sorrow was the widespread adoption of the practice of individual confession. In some parts of the Church, this had been in use for centuries, but its universal adoption took place between 1000 and 1200. At first, confession was very occasional, an affair for the death-bed or to mark some great or unusual event, as when the Empress Agnes made her confession to Peter Damiani on the occasion of a pilgrimage to Rome, but increasingly it came to be a regular feature in the life of the Christian, and in 1215 the fourth Lateran Council imposed annual confession as a minimal obligation upon every member of the Church. The interesting feature of this development is that it was an attempt to introduce the idea of self-examination throughout society; at this point, at least, the pursuit of an interior religion did not remain the property of a small *élite*, but entered every castle and every hovel in western Europe. It is also striking that the theologians of the age laid stress upon confession, not upon priestly absolution, upon personal sincerity, not upon the hierarchy of the Church. Most of them insisted that the absolution merely proclaimed a forgiveness which God had already bestowed because of the good intention of the sinner. This was the opinion, for example, of a twelfth-century preacher: "Those who are cleansed before God are, by the judgement of the priests, shown to men to be clean."[19] The future Pope Alexander III similarly thought that "sin is remitted by contrition of heart".[20] This theology appears to approximate closely to the practice of the time, which regarded confession to a layman as permissible, and indeed desirable, if there were no priest available.[21] On this question at least, Martin Luther would have found little cause for complaint with the Church of the twelfth century.

This concern about inner attitudes is also illustrated by a new stress on intention in the assessment of conduct. To us this point is of such obvious importance that it is surprising to discover how slight was the earlier formal teaching about intention in Western tradition. The most important consideration of the question in classical moral philosophy, in the *Ethics* of Aristotle, was not available in Latin until the thirteenth century, and Germanic society had been generally unaware of the importance of intention. The penal codes usually prescribed punishments for actions and not for the intentions behind them, and the same was true of the Penitentials, where penances were attached to external acts rather than to internal states of mind. As we have seen already, the point had been reached where, after the Battle of Hastings, a penance was imposed without any consideration of the sinner's intention to commit the sin again. It is therefore striking to find that in the early twelfth century, men were keenly aware of the concept of intention, which formed a cardinal feature in the thought of people of varied temperaments. This awareness is another manifestation of the "inwardness" of the time, and we may find its source in the traditional monastic concern with purity of heart, which had blossomed into the strict self-examination which is to be found among the Cluniac monks and Italian hermits.* As has already been mentioned, Guibert of Nogent saw the assessment of intention as a major concern of the historian, and the idea of intention appears frequently in his own work. He returned to it in his discussion of the art of preaching,[22] and in his autobiography he told the story of a suicide who had been misled by the devil, and was forgiven on the intercession of Saint James, who was "mindful of my intention".[23] Bernard of Clairvaux was similarly concerned, not with external actions but with inner motives, and it is hardly too much to say that his whole conception of the spiritual life turned on the intention of the believer, for he saw it as an ascent from the love of God for one's own sake to the love of the

* Traditionally, historians of ethics have stressed the neglect of the idea of intention by the Fathers, and its lack of development until the creative work of Abelard. Although his is certainly the most striking discussion of the subject, I would want to emphasize that the subject was one of general interest among his contemporaries, and that there is more material in monastic tradition on this question than has often been recognized. The picture is therefore one which we find repeated on several occasions: twelfth-century writers recovered and expanded on a theme of earlier monastic thought, and Abelard stated in an extreme form ideas which were cautiously expressed by many other writers.

self for the sake of God: "O holy and chaste love, O sweet and gentle affection, O pure and undefiled intention of the will . . . To be thus disposed is to be united with God."[24] It is interesting to discover that the writers of romances were similarly concerned with a "pure and undefiled intention", although they understood by it something very different. In *The Knight of the Cart* by Chrétien de Troyes, Lancelot is rejected by Guinevere because, when he was summoned to climb on the cart of shame, he hesitated for a moment, thus showing that he was not totally devoted to love of his lady. The force of this passage is not reduced if, as I suspect, Chrétien's purpose was satirical. It was obviously written for an audience which was familiar with the idea of intention, and which could see the point, and possibly the joke, of a lady's demand for a total intention to serve her. The doctrine of intention also entered into the formal theology of the schools. It was emphasized in the school of Laon that every work should be assessed in the light of the intention with which it was begun,[25] but the writer who discussed intention most fully was Abelard, who about 1135 wrote one of his most original works: *Ethics: or, Know Yourself*. For Abelard sin lay solely in the intention. A man could not be called a sinner because he did what was objectively wrong, nor because he felt a sinful desire; sin, purely and simply, lay in consent to sinful desire. The thorough acceptance of the principle "Know yourself" thus led to an ethic of individual intention, and Abelard, who had a remarkable talent for getting himself into trouble, did not hesitate even before the most awkward cases, arguing that those who crucified Jesus were not sinning, because they believed they were acting rightly, a view which horrified Saint Bernard and William of Saint Thierry.* The attempt to make intention the foundation of an ethical theory is a striking instance of the contemporary movement away from external regulations towards an insight into individual character; a movement which finds its widest expression in the acceptance of private confession as the basis of the Church's normal discipline.

---

* For the full statement of Abelard's position on this question, which was rather more subtle than the text (or Saint Bernard) indicate, see D. E. Luscombe, *The School of Peter Abelard* (Cambridge 1969).

THE NEW PSYCHOLOGY

The desire for self-knowledge lay also behind the keen interest which the twelfth century showed in psychology, an interest felt by many different groups. Fashionable society's enthusiasm for the subject was reflected in the inclusion in the romances of passages devoted to discussions of psychology. In the *Cligés* of Chrétien de Troyes, the two lovers of the first half of the novel, Alexander and Soredamors, indulge in lengthy self-questioning about the nature of their feeling for each other, and there are some austere sections about the meaning of common terms—what is meant by giving one's "heart" to another? There was, therefore, a wide concern about psychology, which was also evident in a number of scholars who attempted a thorough examination of the subject. The starting-point here, as so often, was the work of Augustine; but for our purposes we need examine only the modifications and extensions which were made to his system. His idea that man was made in God's image and contained within himself a sort of "little trinity" of memory, reason, and will, fitted ideally the concern of the Cistercians and others to find through self-knowledge the way to God. In another way, however, it was less pleasing to them. Augustine had spent little time on the analysis of motive; all the attractions and emotions of which men were now keenly aware were simply included by him within the "impulse" (*pondus*) which led a man towards good or evil. The particular achievement of the twelfth century was to analyse closely what were called "the affections". This development began about 1100 with Anselm of Canterbury, and continued with William of Saint Thierry (*The Nature and Dignity of Love*, about 1120) and Aelred of Rievaulx (*The Mirror of Charity*, about 1142, and *The Soul*, about 1165). These works did not question the general framework of Augustinian thought, and they accepted that the purpose of psychology was to study the Godward movement of the soul, the things which impeded and encouraged it. It was a "spiritual psychology", or alternatively, in modern terms, a "clinical theology". Above all, they set out to examine whatever *affectus* or *affectio* controlled a man's action. These words described the yearnings for people and things of which every self-conscious man is aware, and may be translated "affection", "disposition", or "appetite". The nature of the affections, and the various kinds of love, were the specific subject of William's treatise *The Nature and Dignity of Love*, and he attempted to create an accepted terminology for this purpose:

> *Affectus* and *affectio* are different from one another. An *affectus* controls the mind with a more or less generalised power, and a more or less permanent strength, stable and lasting, which it obtains by grace. *Affectiones*, however, are themselves varied by the changes of times and events.[26]

The things that most interested William, the examination of the five different kinds of love, lay to a large extent outside the Augustinian scheme, and the same is true of much of Aelred's psychological writing. This change of emphasis has some important implications for the whole understanding of man. It is clear that the thought of these Cistercian writers was theologically motivated and inspired, but they moved away from the older psychology in its essentially simple view of the choice between good and evil. Once the multiplicity of affections and appetites had been recognized, the way lay open both to a better understanding of the individual and to a clearer perception of man's place in the universe. The individual's spiritual progress could be more subtly observed, for there was no longer a stark choice between good (made possible by grace) and evil (if a man is left to himself), but rather there was a variety of appetites and goods. A man may rise from a lesser love to a higher one. All William's five loves may be, in varying degrees, good, and the term *carnalis amor*, which for much of Christian history would have meant fleshly or sinful love, is used to describe love of family, a change of usage which warns us to be careful about our image of the world-renouncing Cistercians. The lesser loves are the stepping-stones to the higher ones; the psychology of the time, however much it was directed towards God as the final goal, had a genuine respect for natural man. Grace did not destroy nature, but perfected it.

By the side of this psychology of the affections there grew up another school of psychology which was eventually to displace the Augustinian scheme entirely. It, too, stressed the study of the passions and affections, but it rested more on the recovery of classical science and less on self-observation; basically, the analysis of the mind was being attempted on the analogy of physical medicine. Such an approach was, it must be admitted, dogged by the inadequacies of Greek science and by the falsity of a simple parallel between body and mind. Its first appearance was in a work by William of Saint Thierry, written in the 1130s, *The Nature of Body and Soul*. The purpose of this book was, like that of *The Nature and Dignity of Love* earlier, to teach self-knowledge as a path to God; indeed, the prologue began with the two foundation-texts of the movement for self-exploration, from Delphi and the Song of Songs. Beside his earlier system William now placed the approach learned from Greek medicine, which had recently been made available through the translation of Saint John of Damascus and others. A passage from book 2 illustrates the character of the new psychology:

> Starting, then, from the mind [*anima*], we must ask what it is, why it is, and how it is ordered. The question what it is, is a medical one; why it is, is a question for reason; how it is ordered is a question for morality. . . . As the body consists of four elements which give it life, so the reasonable mind has four elemental virtues, which are prudence, temperance, fortitude and justice. From these four elements, so to speak, the rationality of the mind is formed. . . . And as the whole nature of the bodily life is centred round three powers, that is, the natural in the liver, the respiratory in the heart and the animal in the brain; so the spiritual and rational use is summed up in three capacities, that is, rationality, concupiscibility and irascibility. . . . To order and complete the spiritual or rational life, there is faith rooted in rationality, hope in concupiscibility, and charity in irascibility.[27]

The crudities involved in this first attempt to digest medical terminology are understandable, and some at least were refined as the system was developed into the psychology which characterized the thirteenth-century schoolmen, and which lasted well into the modern period. For our purposes, it is interesting as showing another face of the twelfth century, its concern with scientific truth, and it is striking that William of Saint Thierry, who was a heated opponent of attempts to give a scientific account of the creation, was the first to welcome a psychology which rested on physical medicine. Although it did not fit happily with the details of his earlier psychology of the affections, it did not as a whole contradict it. It took further the interest in, and concern for, man as a natural being, which had already found expression in the analysis of his affections. The golden rule "Know yourself" led William, first to a psychology resting on self-observation, and then to one constructed on the basis of the physical structure of natural man.

AUTOBIOGRAPHY

The interest in self-exploration led to a further development: autobiography. This was almost unknown in the ancient world. Classical self-expression did not take this form until the *Confessions* of Saint Augustine, which deserve to be called the first autobiography, if by that word we understand an account of the author's life written to illuminate the development of his beliefs and character. For a long time Augustine had no successors, except for some brief accounts written by monks of their conversion to the monastic life (that by Odo of Cluny was incorporated, still in the first person, into John of Salerno's life of him), and for the reminiscences of Ratherius of Verona in the tenth century. From the late eleventh century there is a great increase in the autobiographical content of books on a wide variety of subjects. Suger, abbot of Saint-Denis (1122–51), left descriptions of his political activity, his administration as abbot, and his rebuilding of the abbey church; Aelred of Rievaulx drew on his memories of his friends and of former conversations. The rapidly growing popularity of letter-collections is significant in this connection, for, while they served various purposes, an important reason for their preparation was the opportunity which they gave to the writer or his friends to present his character and opinions to the world. Autobiography was therefore not an isolated phenomenon, but part of general tendency to examine, and publish, one's personal experiences.

Otloh of Saint Emmeram may be regarded as the first autobiographer of the new era. He wrote no formal history of his life, but included a great deal of reminiscence in his numerous books, culminating in a general survey of his own life and works, *On his Temptations and Writings*. Otloh certainly knew Augustine's *Retractations*, and may well have known the *Confessions*, for he wrote a book, which no longer survives, at least as an independent entity, called *The Confession of My Deeds*. It is, however, difficult to believe that it was Augustine's example which stimulated him to autobiography, for the structure of his works is quite different from the *Confessions*, and he was clearly driven to write by the imperative demand of his own inner pressures. He was born a little before 1010 in southern Germany, and was educated at the great monastery of Tegernsee, where he early showed promise as a scholar and as a fine scribe—he taught himself to write privately, and as a result held his pen in a peculiar way. After many hesitations he decided about 1032 to become a monk at Saint Emmeram in Regensburg (Ratisbon). There he remained for the next thirty years, first as head of the school and then as dean, until a series of disputes with the abbot and the bishop came to a head, and he moved to the monastery of Fulda, where he stayed from 1062 to 1066. He died, after returning to Regensburg, about 1070. Superficially his life was isolated from the great movements of the time, and even his very existence is unmentioned outside the books he wrote or composed. We hear nothing from him, for example, of the rising power of the papacy, now launched upon its movement for reform, other than a meeting with Victor II and the formidable Cardinal Humbert, when he heard the latter characteristically saying "much about the insolence of the world, and especially about the negligence of rulers".[28] This apparent obscurity is, however, misleading, for Otloh was a remarkable man, acutely aware of the tensions of his time. His sensitivity drove him into what we would regard as mental illness, and he suffered a series of psychotic episodes, whose course cannot be clearly determined, but which stretched, intermittently at least, from shortly before he became a monk into the late 1050s. Eventually he recovered peace of mind, and was able to give remarkably lucid descriptions of his depressions, dreams, and hallucinations. His disturbances were usually connected with real problems which were troubling him, for Otloh was a man of great and unyielding principle, who never spared himself or others. We are able to see in him the forces which were moving the intellectual world of the eleventh century, felt with abnormal intensity by a particularly sensitive individual.

The first two problems which pressed on him were closely connected in his own mind. Ought he to become a monk? Was it proper for a Christian to read the pagan classics? Otloh had been attracted to the monastic life as a young man at Tegernsee, but he was also a devotee of good literature, especially of Lucan, and he realized that he had hopes of a career as a secular master and scribe, in which he might freely indulge his liking for the classics. These two intertwined problems produced in him a series of disturbing experiences when he was teaching at Saint Emmeram, resident in the guest house and still undecided whether to become a monk. He was particularly distressed by a dream in which he was mercilessly flogged, and he did not know whether or not to take it as a divine warning against the study of pagan literature. While these dreams, and the associated depressions and illnesses, were peculiarly intense, the issues which gave rise to them were real ones, and presented themselves to many people in Otloh's time. The problem of classical literature had been with the Church at least since the time of Saint Jerome, and Otloh's traumatic experiences led him to take up an illiberal position, especially in his early work, *On Spiritual Doctrine*. He was even uneasy whether it was right to have composed it in verse, and he set up a sharp opposition between pagan and Christian learning:

> Avoid the books which tell of worldly lore,
> That you may study sacred letters more.[29]

The problem of vocation was also a growing one at the time. As society became more educated and more complex, able young men were increasingly presented with a choice between becoming a monk and a career in teaching or administration. Otloh's writings reveal the strain which this choice might place upon a deeply conscientious man.

The other issue which distressed Otloh was still more fundamental, and it can best be described in his own words:

> For a long time I found myself tormented by a compulsion to doubt altogether the reliability of Holy Scripture and even the

existence of God himself. When I was troubled by the other temptations indeed, there would be some lucid intervals and some hope of escape, but in these I was deprived for hours on end of any awareness of solace. In the others I was a good deal strengthened by the proofs of Holy Scripture, and fought against the assailing darts of death with the weapons of faith and hope; but on this occasion I was altogether enveloped by complete doubt and darkness of mind, and I thoroughly doubted if there were any truth or profit in the Bible or if Almighty God existed.[30]

This experience underlay his desperate appeal for enlightenment:

Oh, if you indeed exist, Omnipotent, and if you are everywhere present, as I have so often read in many books, now I pray you show your presence and your power, snatching me quickly from the perils about me; for I can no longer bear such great trials.

Otloh himself thought this experience of radical doubt of God's existence quite unheard-of, and there must have been few people in his century, or even in the next one, who felt it with this intensity. None the less, it appears that the grounds for his doubts were difficulties which during the years between 1050 and 1200 troubled a number of thinkers: the doubtful reliability of Scripture, which on occasions contradicted both itself and the Fathers; the demand to know why, if there is a God, he should make a man suffer so much; and the argument that "if Almighty God existed, or had any power, such great confusion and disorder would certainly not be apparent in everything". These considerations were a source of uneasiness to men during our period without, in most cases, creating a serious doubt about God's existence. There is no obvious explanation why, at so early a date, they should be focused so powerfully within the agonized mind of one man; but the experience of Otloh does illuminate the forces which lay under the surface of men's minds, and helps to explain the attempt of Saint Anselm to give a rational justification of faith, and of Abelard to establish the criticism of authority on a sound basis. The tendency to autobiography thus arose in unexpected circumstances, under the impulsion of the inner distress of an unusual man. Its full development is to be found somewhat later in two writers of the early twelfth century, Guibert of Nogent and Peter Abelard.

Guibert spent most of his life inside the cloister. He was probably born in 1053 of a noble family in the region of Beauvais in northern France.* He never knew his father, who was captured shortly before Guibert's birth in a royal expedition against the young Duke William of Normandy, and died in Guibert's infancy. The male element in Guibert's up-bringing was therefore supplied by a resident tutor, whom he later regarded with a mixture of respect and amusement. While still a very young man, Guibert was professed as a monk at Saint-Germer-de-Fly, where he spent many years until his election as abbot of the small monastery of Nogent in 1104. He died about 1123. In this cloistered seclusion, nevertheless, he was a keen observer of the contemporary world. He saw the peasantry setting off for the first Crusade, and described the tragi-comic spectacle of countryfolk nailing shoes to their oxen like horses, loading their children and their few possessions on to their carts, and leaving their homes, while at each castle and village the children eagerly demanded whether this was the Jerusalem for which they sought. He followed the dramatic struggles of near-by towns for communal liberty, and the persecution of the growing heretical movements. He admired the new monastic orders such as the Cistercians and Carthusians; he dedicated a book to Saint Norbert, founder of the Premonstratensians; his studies were directed for a time by the great Anselm, later Archbishop of Canterbury; and he knew and respected the other great Anselm, Master of the school of Laon. He had a wide knowledge of the classics and the Fathers. All these influences are apparent in his writings. His commentary on Genesis shows a grasp of the methods of biblical exposition and of psychology which were being developed at the time. Other works are still more talented and distinctive, for Guibert possessed a critical spirit all his own. His history of the first Crusade, the *Gesta Dei per Francos*, shows remarkable care in the establishment of the facts, and his *Relics of the Saints* (*de pignoribus Sanctorum*) is a fine criticism of a growing, and often disreputable, cult. The *Autobiography* (*Monodiae*)

* See, however, J. F. Benton, *Self and Society*, for a criticism of this date, and also for a bibliography and discussion of Guibert's work.

was completed about 1116. It is something of a scrap-book, but
an intelligent and enjoyable one. The first book is a rather dis-
cursive history of his life up to his election as abbot of Nogent;
the second, a survey of the history of his new abbey; and the third,
a history of the troubles at Laon, with which Guibert was closely
familiar.

Unnoticed by Guibert, the city of Laon had about 1113 briefly
received a remarkable visitor in the brilliant Peter Abelard, who
had come to study theology under Master Anselm. Endowed with
many talents, Abelard came close to being the "universal man"
beloved of a later age. A brilliant teacher, logician, philosopher,
theologian, hymn-writer, and autobiographer, and a famous lover,
he also won golden opinions from some by his devotion as a
monk. His restless and troubled career defies brief summary. His
autobiography takes the form of a very long letter to an unnamed
friend, variously entitled *Letter of Consolation* and *History of his
Calamities*, and was written about 1131–5. In all surviving manuscripts it is followed by a correspondence arising from it between
Abelard and Heloïse, his former mistress and wife, who by then
was Abbess of the Holy Paraclete, which Abelard had founded for
her. The letters are remarkably revealing on both sides, although
their authenticity has been repeatedly questioned—not, it seems
to me, convincingly.

These autobiographies are rooted in repentance and self-
examination. They are "confessions" in both senses of the word:
a confession of the writer's sin and of the just judgements of God.
Guibert, who was taking Augustine's *Confessions* as his exemplar,
thus described the object of his work: "Thou knowest, most
merciful God, that I began this work not in the spirit of pride, but
wishing to confess my wickedness, which I would most plainly
acknowledge, did I not fear to corrupt the minds of many by my
horrible acts."[31] Abelard, while he was not obviously influenced
by the *Confessions*, had a similar purpose in writing, and regarded
his misfortunes as an appropriate punishment for his lechery and
pride. In a sense, therefore, these books, so far from being an
expression of interest in the individual, are designed to point
away from him to God; to say "not unto us, O Lord, but unto thy
name give the praise". Yet they are still works of genuine self-

revelation. Partly this is because both writers were convinced that God had manifested himself in the maturing of their experience and understanding; and they were, in fact, men of real perception about themselves. Guibert's account of his appearance before Pope Paschal II at Langres in 1107, to defend the election of the deplorable Gaudri as bishop of Laon, is a masterpiece of honest and satirical self-observation. His successful conduct of the defence consisted, on his own showing, of a series of half-truths, gross flatteries, and smooth evasions; as Guibert delicately put it, "not entirely deviating from the truth".[32] There was also another element in the birth of autobiography which contributed much to its vitality and individuality: the author's pride in his works. In the twelfth century poets, sculptors, and scribes all began to show a keen appreciation of the merits of their own works—witness a psalter produced at Canterbury about 1150, in which Eadwine, the scribe or designer, wrote around a picture of himself: "I am the prince of writers; neither my fame nor my praise will die quickly . . . Fame proclaims you in your writing for ever, Eadwine, you who are to be seen here in the painting."[33]

Guibert and Abelard both took their work very seriously. Guibert, by a trick, obtained his abbot's permission to write a Commentary on Genesis, and when the permission was withdrawn he continued the work in secret. The episode is narrated in his *Autobiography* without the least suggestion that it was odd behaviour for a monk bound by a vow of obedience. Such a degree of self-confidence made for a readiness to criticize others. While Guibert had considerable affection for his former schoolmaster, his critical pen has provided us with a portrait which stands high in the long tradition of schoolboy reminiscence:

The love that this man had for me was a savage sort, and he showed too much severity in his undeserved beatings; and yet the great care with which he guarded me was evident in his acts. Clearly I did not deserve to be beaten, for if he had had the skill in teaching which he professed, it is certain that I was, as a boy, well able to grasp anything that he taught correctly. But because he did not say what he meant and what he tried to express was not at all clear to himself, his talk rolled on and on ineffectively in a circle, trundling along without direction, and could not arrive at any conclusion, let alone be understood. For he was so ill-instructed that he remembered incorrectly what he had, as I explained earlier, learnt badly late in life, and if he inadvertently let something slip out, he would maintain and defend it with blows, regarding all his own opinions as certainly true.[34]

As to Abelard, no one ever managed to prevent him from saying what he thought, and his consciousness of his own faults did not make him charitable to the faults of others. His account of Master Anselm of Laon, so revered throughout France, is startling:

> I came therefore to this old man, who owed his reputation to long habit rather than intelligence or memory. If anybody came knocking at his door in perplexity about some problem, he would go away still more perplexed. He was wonderful in the eyes of his admirers, but in the sight of those who asked questions he was no one. He had a marvellous flow of words, but its meaning was trivial and its reasoning empty. When he lit his fire, he filled his house with smoke, but produced no light.[35]

The whole of the *Letter of Consolation* has a sweet-sour taste. Abelard was striving to overcome that arrogant brilliance which had won him so many enemies, but its glitter can be seen in almost every paragraph, whether he is ascribing his keen intellect to the climate of his native Britanny, or explaining to his readers that his fame and beauty were such that no woman could have refused him. Guibert's *Autobiography* and Abelard's *Letter of Consolation* are vivid self-portraits in an age which had come to value individuality.

THE PORTRAIT

Most ages have made representations of their great men, for varying purposes and in different media: in stone or on canvas, on seals or coins. Such portraits have both a private and a public aspect. Men are still depicted today showing their insignia of public status, in academic gown or mayoral chain. On the whole, however, we are now more interested in the portrait as a record of the individual. We hope to find in it a personal likeness and, in the work of a perceptive painter, some expression of his character. Such, at least, has been the tradition of portraiture until the present century, but it has not been universal in the past, and in particular European art in the centuries after the fall of the Roman Empire was more concerned with rank and status than with recording personal features.

Art historians have sometimes approached this question by making a distinction between a picture and a portrait, or more strictly, since the great majority of discussions are in German, between *Bildnis* and *Porträt*. The distinction may seem to us a sensible one, separating as it does a picture intended to convey an idea, of (for instance) Christ or the Emperor, from one which represents the individual in his distinctive characteristics, but it does not correspond with anything in medieval usage, for such contemporary words as *imago* and *pictura* do not carry this connotation. More seriously, to separate absolutely pictures from portraits is to misunderstand what the artists of the time probably thought they were doing. In all portraiture there is a projection of the artist's image of his subject, and tenth-century painters clearly thought that they were depicting the Emperor, even if they were impressed by (or in a sense "saw") the symbols of imperial majesty rather than the physical features of the young Otto. To insist that they must have been painting either a picture or a portrait forces upon the art of the time a doctrinaire division which did not exist in reality. The process which took place in the centuries after A.D. 1000 was the inclusion of more and more personal details in a portrait, and our present task is to assess the speed and extent of this process. It is therefore essential to avoid a terminology which prevents us from seeing this as a continuing process, and at the risk of some artificiality I therefore intend to use the word "portrait" to describe any contemporary representation of a particular person, and the term "personal portrait" with the narrower meaning of a portrait which in our everyday sense looks like the subject. In a personal portrait you would know the subject if you saw him in his bath. Thus defined, we have to study the personalization of the portrait: not an abrupt adoption of a new way of painting, but a steady transformation of vision.

We must admit from the beginning that it is not possible to be certain, with any portrait before 1200, that it is in our sense a personal study.* It is this uncertainty which accounts for the extreme variation in views which have been expressed by modern writers. One position is that of Harald Keller in a study with the uncompromising title *The Origin of the Portrait in the Later Middle Ages*:

> The portrait, as we understand it today, is one of the new concepts of the late Middle Ages . . . The characterization of a man absolutely and unchangeably by his particular physical peculiarities, especially his face, and not by the insignia of his office or rank or by his weapons—that is a concept of the portrait which in the second century A.D. came into question in the West, and which was progressively lost from the time of Constantine onwards. Only about 1300 did the new conception of man lead to the recovery of the old idea of the portrait.[36]

Even confining this description to the period from A.D. 500 to 1000, it is too absolute to accept without qualification. The basic idea that a portrait was intended to be an identifiable likeness never died altogether, and during this long period there were several instances of artists inspired by classical examples to attempt a life-like rendering of their subject.† All the same, Keller is un-

---

* The full discussion of any particular case would obviously occupy a considerable amount of space, but the difficulties in brief are these. We do not usually have more than a small number of portraits definitely ascribed to a named person, in particular a king. Manuscript illuminations are often too small to provide a personal likeness; seal images and coins are also often too small, and by their very nature they stress symbols of office; they were even at times retained unchanged by a successor. Statues have usually lost their colouring, and have worn features—the very things by which a personal likeness is easily recognized. Moreover, similarities may be stylistic or ideological, and not indicate the individual's real features. When all these uncertainties are remembered, it will be appreciated that conclusions need to be cautious.

† There are several instances in Carolingian art where, inspired by classical example, the artist produces a distinct individual likeness, al-though we have no means of knowing whether it is a personal portrait of the subject. An interesting case is the coinage of Offa, cast in highly classical style and in a quality so fine that a strong individual likeness is

doubtedly right in thinking that the interest of painters during this period was much more focused on office than on individual appearance. The portraits of Otto III (983–1002) in the liturgical manuscripts which he sponsored provide an interesting case in point, because some of them give him an extremely distinctive appearance, the face of a youthful visionary. Since it is probable enough that Otto was known to the scribes of these imperial books, one is tempted to regard these as personal portraits. But the conclusion would be a hazardous one. Otto's features are similar to those of Christ in other compositions, and it may well be that the portraits were intended to display Otto as a manifestation of Christ, not to record his individual appearance. Another portrait of him, at Aachen where he was personally known, is totally dissimilar, and it is a striking fact that when the illuminator of such a manuscript heard of his patron's death, he modified the Emperor's portrait by the simple expedient of writing above it the name of his successor, Heinrichus, in spite of the fact that Henry II was much older than Otto.[37] Similarly, in a codex of about 983 the scribe Anno drew himself in the act of presenting the book to Archbishop Gero of Cologne. The figures are almost identical except for their dress and size, Gero being much the larger as became his higher rank.[38] About the year 1000, therefore, it is safe to say that artists were little, if at all, concerned with the recording of individual likenesses. At the other end of the process, before 1300 we have royal tomb figures which are unquestionably personal portraits, and sculptors had begun to work from death-masks, thus attempting personal portraiture of a very exact kind. The tomb-figure of Louis of France, the eldest son of Saint Louis, who predeceased his father in 1260, is highly life-like, and may plausibly be regarded as an early example of this approach.[39] It is probable that the fine statue of Henry III (died 1272) at Westminster was worked from his death-mask, and it is certain that the sculpture at Cosenza of Isabel, wife of Philip III of France, was, for her face is gashed and distorted from the fall which killed her on the way back from the Tunis Crusade in 1270.[40] Between about 1000 and

---

clear in several of his coins. It has in fact been called the "portrait coinage", but whether the features are those of Offa, or of the coiners' classical model, is a sheer matter of guesswork.

1260, therefore, there lies a movement from a portraiture which concentrated on hierarchy and station, to one which was keenly aware, at least on occasions, of personal appearance.*

The twelfth century saw a distinct shift in the visual arts towards sensitivity to nature, and a more characteristically modern way of seeing the human form. Ottonian art had made its impact through insignia, symbols, posture, and colour. While these devices were by no means abandoned, more stress came to be placed upon the human form and features. The idea of kingliness was conveyed through the nobility, benevolence, or severity of the figure's expression, as in some of the sculptures of the new Gothic cathedrals. The figure of Eve, carved at Autun before the middle of the century by its great sculptor Gislebert, has been called the first seductive female in Western art since the fall of Rome, and if the claim is a large one, it contains a good deal of truth. This movement towards naturalism was sometimes accompanied by a delight in personal gestures and in private idiosyncrasies. Scribes might on occasion become quite skittish. About 1150 Hildebert, a lay scribe working at Prague, sketched himself and his apprentice Everwin in two manuscripts, in one of which they are chasing away a mouse which is stealing their lunch.[41] It would be too much to call these little drawings personal portraits, but they display the interest in individual character and circumstance which is a preliminary to personal portraiture.

The best field in which to look for formal portraits in the twelfth century is in memorial- or tomb-sculpture. Such pictures are virtually unknown before 1080, but from that time they become progressively more common. In the cloisters of the Abbey of Moissac was placed a sculpture of Abbot Durand, who had been responsible for extensive building there. It was probably executed a little before 1100 and therefore some twenty years after his death, but it is a clear and naturalistic carving. One can only guess whether

* This is not in any way to deny that the portraits of important men continued to incorporate large elements of imagery, symbolic of their status. The liturgical and thematic content of the portrait has recently been the subject of an interesting study by K. Hoffman, *Taufsymbolik im mittelalterlichen Herrscherbild* (Düsseldorf 1968). The continued vitality of imagery does not exclude the possibility of a keener eye for personal features.

it looks like the original Durand, but it is worth recording that the great art critic Marcel Aubert regarded it as unquestionably a personal portrait.[42] From this time onwards we find a series of enamel plaques probably designed as memorials, which sometimes carry laudatory inscriptions and depict faces of great individuality, such as the formidable portrait of Geoffrey Plantagenet (d. 1151)* now at Le Mans. Late in the century there is apparent a concern to record in a natural and accurate way the circumstances of a funeral. It is likely that Henry II (d. 1189) was the first king of England to be carried to burial, not under a pall, but with his face uncovered and his body clothed in coronation robes. The tomb figure at Fontevrault† shows the king lying in his robes of state. The effigy of King John (d. 1216) at Worcester[43] is still more clearly a case in point, for when the tomb was opened the skeleton was found in almost the identical, and distinctive, position of the sculpture. In a number of ways, therefore, interest was demonstrably shifting towards naturalistic representation and the depiction of individual characteristics. It is more difficult to say how far this had led to personal portraiture as I have defined it. It may seem a matter of common sense that, when portraits become more individual, the artist must be depicting the actual appearance of the person concerned, but in making such an assumption we are perhaps misled by the approach of our own age. The portrait of Geoffrey Plantagenet is distinctive enough, but it is not clear whether the artist intended to provide an "ideal" representation of his forceful subject, or whether Count Geoffrey did in fact have just such hair and features as we see in the portrait. The tomb figure of Henry II at Fontevrault shows him as younger than he was at his death, and that of his consort Eleanor of Aquitaine, who died in her eighties, is that of a middle-aged woman. If they are personal portraits at all, they are romanticized ones. In other words, a naturalistic or individualistic portrait is not necessarily a genuinely personal one in the strict sense, although in many cases it may be.

The personalization of the portrait can perhaps best be illustrated by considering two portraits of German kings. The earlier is the tomb figure of Rudolf of Suabia at Merseburg.‡ Rudolf had been

* Plate 2.   † Plate 4.   ‡ Plate 1.

elected anti-king on behalf of the papacy against the excommuni-
cate Emperor Henry IV. On his death in battle in 1080 he was
regarded by the Church as a martyr, and received a bronze
memorial upon his tomb, a tribute which may well have been
unique at the time. An inscription told of his virtues:

> In this tomb is buried King Rudolf, who died for the law of the
> fathers, and is rightly to be mourned. No king since Charle-
> magne was his equal, in counsel or battle, had he but reigned
> in time of peace. Where his men triumphed, he, war's sacred
> victim, fell. For him, death was life. He died for the church.

The memorial marks a stage in the definition of that ideal of
chivalry which saw the warrior as God's servant. It also shows the
reaction of the men of the time to someone whose position was
highly unusual. Rudolf was not simply a model of kingship, for
he had intervened in the cause of the Church against the anointed
king. In this context it would be natural to expect a visual emphasis,
not on the symbols of kingship, but rather upon personal characteristics. Commentators have differed on whether the bronze casting
should be regarded as a personal portrait. While powerful, it is
also clumsy: the body incised flat on the slab, the head alone given
three-dimensional treatment, the mouth treated as a long curved
line. On the other hand, the special treatment of the head presumably reveals a particular interest in the features. The artist saw the
face in the abstract linear terms which naturally appealed to the
eleventh-century eye, but handled it in such a way as to produce a
powerful and moving composition. It is tempting to accept the
view of Hubert Schrade,[44] that we have here an attempt at a
personal portrait by an artist whose vision still did not extend to a
truly naturalistic rendering. He is, I think, trying to present the
character of an individual through these features; whether they
in any way resemble the actual physical appearance of the historical
Rudolf cannot be decided, for no other portrait survives which is
of any use as a check. The very personal character of his situation
tempts one to think that it may have been expressed by a real
approach towards a personal portrait, but to say so is to guess.
The second portrait which we should consider is the famous

Cappenberg head representing the Emperor Frederick Barbarossa.*
It was a gift from Frederick to his godfather, Count Otto of
Cappenberg. Otto, having joined the monastery there, subsequently gave the head to the Church to act as a reliquary, describing it in his deed of gift as "made in the likeness of the Emperor".
The survival of a piece of treasure of this sort is unusual, and the
head is unique in that it is specifically said to be a portrait of one
particular person; and from these facts its importance in the history
of portraiture arises. It was made of gilded bronze between 1155
and 1171. It has considerable elements of the symbolic, and also of
the conventional. The stand probably represents Rome, and
Frederick's lordship over the imperial city. The elements of the
face, considered from the naturalistic standpoint, are imperfect:
the mouth too small, the eyebrows are strict semi-circles, and the
tight curls of hair are not realistic. The band or fillet is imitated
from the busts of late Roman emperors, and so is the distinctive
haircut. All this having been said, it is also obvious that the general
approach is naturalistic, and that the transformation of an abstract
and linear vision into the presentation of individual character,
which was perhaps beginning in the portrait of Rudolf of Suabia,
has clearly made great progress. We can see here a man who com-
bines pride of birth with that knightly elegance and affability
which was increasingly valued in the society of the time. The man
who designed this portrait certainly liked to depict individual
traits of character. Can we go further and say that this is a genuinely
personal portrait, that Barbarossa really "looked like that"?

A comparison of the head with other portraits of Barbarossa
is inconclusive in its results. The very fine set of imperial and
royal bulls and seals, probably designed by the outstanding gold-
smith Godfrey de Huy, do not give much facial detail, and defeat

* Plate 3. For a full discussion, with details of literature, see H. Grundmann, *Der Cappenberger Barbarossakopf und die Anfänge des Stiftes
Cappenberg* (Cologne 1959). Some scholars have held that the bust was a
purely personal gift, without political or liturgical significance, and that
it therefore may reasonably be regarded as an individual likeness and
nothing more. This view seems to me indefensible (see, for example,
K. Hoffmann, *Taufsymbolik im mittelalterlichen Herrscherbild* (Düsseldorf
1968) pp. 82–8) and in the text I have taken the more cautious position
that there is a mingling of traditional symbolism with personal likeness.

us by their very excellence, for they were retained in use, not only throughout Frederick's reign, but also, with minimal adaptation, for the wax seal of his successor Henry VI—a fact which warns us that, if the personal portrait was possibly in use in some forms of art, it was not considered obligatory on official seals.[45] The seals do, however, show Barbarossa as having curly hair, an attribute which also appears on the arm-reliquary of Charlemagne and on other portraits, and which is sufficiently unusual for us to accept it as a genuinely personal feature. Other portraits also confirm the general facial type, and particularly the long and striking nose, but their evidence is not firm enough to come to a secure conclusion. More convincing is the series of literary descriptions of Frederick, in particular that of Rahewin:

> He had blond hair, curled a little way back from the forehead. His ears were barely covered by the hair over them, because (out of reverence for the Empire) the barber kept short the hair of his head and face with regular cutting. He had sharp and penetrating eyes; a fine nose, reddish beard, a small mouth with well-shaped lips, and his whole expression was happy and gay.

Rahewin was undoubtedly selecting those features of Frederick's appearance which were appropriate to his idea of him as a monarch and a knight, and if the Cappenberg head did not exist, one might even be sceptical enough to regard it as a purely ideal description. The similarity between this passage and the Cappenberg portrait, however, is so close that it is impossible to doubt that both are personal descriptions of the same individual, and it is particularly interesting to observe that the "imperial" hairstyle shown on the bust, which we might otherwise have supposed was an artist's classical reminiscence, was in fact affected by Frederick.

The Cappenberg head is unique in its kind in that both the work of art itself, and the name of the subject, have survived. Were there many personal portraits originally in this period, now lost to us? It would be incautious to assume that they were ever very numerous. Frederick was particularly likely to inspire a work of this kind, and there are more verbal descriptions of his appearance, and more portraits of him (though none of them the equal of the Cappenberg head) than of any other twelfth-century figure. He also encouraged classical imitation, and the head was one of the results of this. Even in Hohenstaufen circles, as we have seen, seals did not necessarily bear a personal portrait; and the evidence is indecisive as to whether tomb-sculptures were yet personal portraits. A safe conclusion, although it may err on the side of caution, would be to say that the twelfth century saw a marked move towards a more individual treatment of the portrait, which began increasingly to display details of appearance and personality. In certain circles artists arrived at a genuine personal portraiture, and in the Cappenberg head the age has left us a record of the appearance of one of its most remarkable men.

5 The Self and other Selves

God is Friendship
AELRED OF RIEVAULX

Man without love is little worth
BERNARD OF VENTADOUR

The growth of a keen self-awareness was naturally accompanied by a fresh interest in close personal relationships. The twelfth century has been called the century of friendship, and it occupies an important, if controversial, place in the history of the Western idea of sexual love. In some senses we are likely to find this aspect of the age genuinely "modern", because our own century has been marked by a growing disillusion with large political or religious solutions and the attachment of a higher value to the relationship of person to person. We must therefore beware of the danger of importing into the twelfth century assumptions which are natural to us, but would have been entirely foreign to them, for the character of friendship and love, and the language in which they were expressed, differed a great deal from our own experience. The two things both drew upon a conventional stock of imagery, and the language used often rings strangely in our ears. Friends spoke in words which now sound erotic, and lovers not infrequently sound formal and stilted. Modern readers of the letters of Anselm of Canterbury and the poems of Jaufre Rudel have sometimes concluded that the monk was in love with his friend, and the poet not in love with his lady. The mistake is understandable, for their imagery has changed its meaning. On the one hand, friendship could be given a more physical expression than in modern Britain; the "kiss of friendship" would be given in actual fact, and the symbol of the kiss or embrace might therefore express affection rather than sensuality. Conversely, the troubadours' desire to serve their ladies, which sometimes appears to us to lack warmth, had a strongly erotic content. They were often thinking of the role of personal servant, charged with the care of their mistress' clothes and person. I shall have to return later to these two themes, passion in friendship and service in love; they are mentioned now simply to alert the reader to the care needed in understanding twelfth-century imagery.

The literatures of friendship and love developed in different circles, for the one was characteristic of the monastery, the other of the lay courts. It is true that there was an important overlap between the two cultures in the writing of the Latin humanists. Men such as Baudri of Bourgueil would write poems or letters of friendship, but he also knew his Ovid, and could compose a delicate poem of amorous flattery. There is indeed no shortage of love poetry in Latin, and some at least of the vernacular love poets were influenced by the culture of the schools. But the instances of writers who made an important contribution both to the literature of friendship and of love are few,* and it is better to discuss the two movements separately.

FRIENDSHIP

The characteristic vehicle for declarations of friendship was the letter. Although letter-collections have been made in every literate age, the importance attached to them had perhaps never been as great as it was in the twelfth century. We still possess collections of the correspondence of many of the great men of the age: Bernard of Clairvaux, Anselm of Canterbury, Peter the Venerable, Hildebert of Lavardin, and Peter of Blois, to mention only a few. In character, these letters vary from the moving and intimate exchanges of Abelard and Heloïse to the businesslike file of Gilbert Foliot. The epistolary form was borrowed for works which were not really letters at all; Abelard's autobiography is

---

* The most striking instances are Abelard and Heloïse, but here the exception proves the rule, for their relations were very unusual, Heloïse being in turn Abelard's mistress, wife, and spiritual daughter. Their manifold relationship was movingly described by Heloïse in the address of one of her letters: "Domino suo, imo patri; conjugi suo, imo fratri; ancilla sua, imo filia; ipsius uxor, imo soror. Abaelardo Heloissa."

supposed to be a letter of consolation to a friend, but one suspects
that this is only a stylistic device. A great deal of what we know
about the ideal of friendship comes from these collections of
letters. Friendship was, indeed, of such concern to them that it
spilled into other types of literature. It was the subject of a good
deal of poetry, and it invaded the sermon—the most famous of all
friendship-sermons, Bernard's lament on the death of his brother
Gerard, was mentioned in the last chapter. Friendship also
inspired a few formal treatises, and it is worth remembering that
our knowledge of Aelred, one of the great apostles of friendship,
comes from his book on the subject and his biographer's description. Aelred's own letter-collection, which we know to have
existed at one time, has unhappily been lost.

There was already a long tradition of learned thought about
friendship, a tradition which ascribed to it many of the values
which we ascribe to marriage. The classical philosophers sought a
community of mind and spirit not with their wives, but with
their friends. The West did not at this time know the discussions
of friendship by Plato and Aristotle, and classical teaching on the
subject came to them through the epistles of Seneca, and still
more through Cicero's attractive dialogue, *de Amicitia*, which was
probably the best loved of any book by a non-Christian author.
The cult of friendship had been taken up by the Fathers of the
Church, who were attracted to it partly because they were celibate,
and therefore looked naturally to friendship as an ideal, and
partly because of the elements in the Scriptures which encouraged
a Christian theory and practice of friendship. The Old Testament
offered the example of David and Jonathan, the perfect friends;
the New Testament contained teaching about the friendship of
Christ. The ideas of Cicero were therefore taken up by Jerome,
Ambrose, and Cassian, who left to subsequent generations an
ideal of friendship which contained strong Christian overtones,
and which in a sense was the basis of a spiritual way of life. This
tradition did not die out at any time, and was a marked feature of
the Carolingian Renaissance, but it was seized upon most eagerly
of all by the men of the twelfth century. Its attractions were many.
It provided an ideal for the new, international class of intellectuals,
who had no structural or accepted part in society; we shall see

later that it provided them with at once an object in life and a mode of international co-operation. It appealed to the new monastic orders, whose more intense members, all of whom had consciously rejected the world, found in it a satisfying definition of a new relationship within the community. The ideal of friendship was closely connected with the exploration of the self and the search for a true identity, for it thus provided scholars and monks with a sense of community, based upon a humane ideal of personal relations. We encounter once again the paradox that some of the movements most devoted to world-rejection, such as the Cistercians, were at the same time the champions of humanist attitudes.

A complete account of friendship in the twelfth century would have to recognize that each writer has his own tone and his particular approach to the subject. These varied according to the author's position in society (a scholar such as Hildebert inevitably writes somewhat differently from a monk); according to the genre of literature in which he was working (a treatise is one thing, a letter another); and according to his personal temperament. We can observe the passionate declarations of love to which Anselm of Canterbury was given; the conscious classical and patristic reminiscences in Hildebert's letters; the generous tolerance of Peter the Venerable; and the golden pen of Bernard of Clairvaux, which covers a realism which is at times impressive, and at other times distasteful.* In spite of these differences the friendship writers shared an ideal which was held with remarkable unity all over western Europe, a unity due in part to the fidelity which they showed to the classical and patristic tradition, and in part to the remarkably international outlook of the writers, whose correspondence covered great distances to the furthest parts of Western Christendom. It is therefore reasonable to treat the cult of friendship essentially as one ideal, and to see how it was practised in the social conditions of the twelfth century. Before

---

* For example, Bernard's last letter to Abbot Suger of Saint-Denis is so moving in its expression that the reader almost fails to notice that he is refusing to visit his dying friend: "Perhaps I shall come, perhaps I shall not. But whatever happens I, who have loved you from the first, shall love you without end" (tr. B. S. James, no. 411).

examining it as a system it would be worth while to consider one particular example, a man whose gift for friendship was outstanding even among his contemporaries.

Aelred of Rievaulx is interesting for several reasons. His importance as a personality and thinker is a relatively recent discovery; his life was led far from the centres of French culture, at Hexham, Durham, the court of David of Scotland, and Rievaulx, and it is striking to find how deeply the north of England had been influenced by international learning; and we know a good deal about his development and personal relations both from his own reminiscences and his biography by Walter Daniel. Aelred found from his youth that he formed strong personal attachments, and his discovery of Cicero's *de Amicitia* in his student days was a source of great delight to him. He may conceivably have been influenced on this point by a friend of his family, Lawrence of Durham, a southern Englishman who had joined the cathedral priory at Durham and who eventually presented his copy of the *de Amicitia* to the library there; one wonders (although this is mere speculation) if this was the very copy which the young Aelred read. As a steward in the household of David of Scotland, he was closer to international learned circles than may at first appear. David was engaged in the active Normanization of Scotland, and was a firm friend and favourite of his uncle, Henry I of England, whose court, with its wide connections in western Europe, he visited for long periods in 1126 and 1130. In 1134, when he decided to join the Cistercian community at Rievaulx, Aelred moved into a group with still stronger links with Europe, for the monks had arrived from France only two years previously. Aelred visited Clairvaux in 1142 and met Saint Bernard, who was so impressed that he urged him to write his first book, *The Mirror of Charity*. This contains a considerable amount about friendship, but his most formal discussion is to be found in his later book, *Spiritual Friendship*. This was one of the few full-scale treatises on the subject, and it impressed Peter of Blois sufficiently in the next generation for him to plagiarize large sections of it without acknowledgement. *Spiritual Friendship* was written in stages between 1150 and 1165; the participant in the first dialogue, Ivo, had died before the second part of the book was composed. It is a humane book, in its presentation as well as its subject-matter, for the characters of Aelred's friends are adroitly portrayed in their conversation, particularly that of Walter, faithful and affectionate but also jealous and slightly resentful. It shows a deep and close knowledge of Cicero's *de Amicitia*, and considerable parts of the book are a quotation and amplification of Cicero. The contribution made by Aelred to friendship did not lie in his originality, for his ideas may be seen as part and parcel of the twelfth-century thought about the subject. It is rather the large role which he assigned to it, for it is scarcely an exaggeration to say that he saw the whole aim of the spiritual life to lie in friendship. He remarked that, as he moved through his monastery, he felt himself in paradise, bound to all his brethren by bonds of friendship.[1] Walter Daniel has left a vivid and moving account of the love which united Aelred with his monks, particularly during his last years, when he was confined by an excruciating illness to a specially built cell or sick-bed:

> The construction of this cot was, indeed, a great source of consolation to the brethren, for every day they came to it and sat in it, twenty or thirty at a time, to talk together of the spiritual delights of the Scriptures and of the observance of the Order. There was nobody to say to them, "Get out, go away, do not touch the Abbot's bed"; they walked and lay about his bed and talked with him as a child prattles with its mother. He would say to them, "My sons, say what you will; only let no vile word, no detraction of a brother, no blasphemy against God proceed out of your mouth".

This easy intimacy contrasts remarkably with the more passionate, but more abstract, declarations of Saint Anselm, although it is necessary to remind ourselves that we do not possess Aelred's letters, which may well have been like Anselm's in tone, and also that Rievaulx ran into difficulties after Aelred's death—he must have been an impossible man to succeed, and one's sympathy goes out to the next abbot.[2] In thinking of friendship as one of the highest emotional satisfactions possible to man, and as the road to an understanding of God, Aelred did not fundamentally differ from his contemporaries, but shared in his own way an experience which at its heart was common to them all.

There was, in their eyes, nothing trivial or superficial about friendship, for it rested upon a common concern for fundamentals. Three texts were regularly quoted, or echoed. There was the definition of Cicero: "Friendship is nothing other than a common mind [*consensio*] in divine and human things, with benevolence and charity."[3] There was also Sallust's definition of friendship as "to love and to hate the same things",[4] and the verse in the Acts of the Apostles: "Now the company of those who believed were of one heart and soul, and no one said that any of the things which he possessed was his own, but they had everything in common" (Acts 4.32). A relationship of this deep kind could arise in the normal course of life between two colleagues who respected one another, but it might also be established more formally. Just as in lay society there had been the custom of taking a sworn companion, or *compainz*, so in monastic circles one could form a sworn friendship. Peter the Venerable often referred to the oath which tied him to a friend, and the process may be observed in a letter written in the late 1120s to Bernard of Clairvaux by Hildebert, then archbishop of Tours:

> From all that I have heard of you I have come to love you, and to desire with a great desire to be admitted to the sanctuary of your friendship, and remembered by you when you steal from converse with men to speak to the King of angels on behalf of men.[5]

Bernard's answer was an acceptance: "Such as I am, I am yours". An undertaking of this sort was envisaged as involving a life-long commitment. Cicero had taught that "true friendships are eternal",[6] and the combination of a vow and of an eternal bond led to language which to our ears belongs to romantic love. Saint Bernard wrote to Hugh of Prémontré:

> For my part, I am determined to love you whatever you do, even if you do not return my love . . . I shall cling to you, even against your will; I shall cling to you, even against my own will. Once I bound myself to you with a strong bond, with charity unfeigned, that charity which never fails.[7]

A favourite theme with Saint Bernard was the importance of accepting a man as he is, and of not treating him as a creation of one's own imagination:

> You could reach me if you but considered what I am; and you can reach me still whenever you wish, if you are content to find me as I am and not as you wish me to be. I cannot think what else you see in me besides what I am, what it is you are chasing which is not me.[8]

Accordingly, it was generally recognized that it was a duty to be completely open with a friend; a duty which, to judge by the number of bitter complaints made in the name of friendship, sometimes became a pleasure. Ideally this openness and acceptance should lead to a deep unity of purpose with the other, who became, as Horace put it, "half of my soul",[9] a theme taken up by Lawrence of Durham:

> Dear friend,
> Part of my soul, I feel that I myself
> Am bitterly divided in your death.

Close to this was another frequently expressed idea, that friends are not divided by distance, since their unity lies in the mind and will. Hildebert wrote to a friend: "Perhaps you do not know it, but I was with you at Rome. With you I suffered the oppressive snow, with you endured the mountains, glittering with ice or sharp with rocks. I bore them all with you, for I grieved when you bore them."[10]

At its best, the practice of friendship contained those insights of acceptance and honesty which we value today; but it remains odd, in our eyes, that these ideas should be expressed between men who, as far as personal acquaintanceship went, were really strangers to each other. Yet it would be a great mistake to suppose that we have here an artificiality, a literary game of cultured men. Such friendships were very relevant to the conditions of contemporary life. They were designed partly to secure fellowship in prayer. This was a practical question in the mind of the men of the time, and was the only specific request contained in Hildebert's letter proposing friendship with Bernard. Moreover, the practice of friendship had the effect of creating a network all over western Europe linking men of common mind. Hildebert was fond of insisting that for those united in friendship all places were one commonwealth, and the existence of a "commonwealth of friendship" provided its members with both an inspiration and a basis for political action. The humanists and reformers of the twelfth century, like those of the early sixteenth, were eager for reform in both Church and State, and the possibility of this depended essentially on their ability to make their views heard in the papal Curia and in royal and baronial courts. To win friends and to influence people was half the battle, and correspondence with a wide range of friends was fundamental to their attempt to control policy. These connections could be used to "place" sympathizers, as when Saint Bernard wrote to Archbishop Theobald of Canterbury to recommend John of Salisbury, "a friend of me and of my friends".[11] They could be a potent political weapon. In the schism of 1130 the victory of Innocent II in the north of Europe was mainly due to a group of people who appear to have been in close touch with one another: Saint Bernard, Saint Norbert, Peter the Venerable, and the papal chancellor Haimeric. On occasions such friendship-networks could be employed ruthlessly as pressure groups, but they could also bring encouragement and help to remarkably wide circles of people. Peter the Venerable was by reputation (as Bernard handsomely put it) "the man whom all desire to have as their advocate".

Just as the cult of friendship was of direct relevance to the political and religious conditions of the day, so it unquestionably meant a great deal personally to the friends. We must remember that a letter was a considerable present, involving trouble and expense in its preparation and its delivery, and to receive an open letter from a great literary or spiritual figure must have been an honour and pleasure to anyone. The emotions involved appear in a letter to Peter the Venerable from Bishop Atto of Trier, whose dry tone persuades us that we are hearing his real feelings:

> True friendship knows no forgetfulness, nor does it suffer interruption . . . I am happy to believe that there is in you the same spirit of love, but I would be happier if I were sure.

For there is something which I can no longer conceal, which friendship compels me to speak aloud. God! Where are the frequent letters, where is the regular solace, where is the accustomed eloquence, with which you used to comfort your friend in his old age? But I suppose you cannot find a pen, or the ink has gone, or there are no messengers, or the way is mountainous, or the dangers are too great. A hint is enough for a wise man.[12]

Conversely, the delight in hearing from a friend appears in a letter of Bernard's, also to Peter:

When your letter first arrived, I was only able to take a short, but very affectionate, glance at it. I was busy at the time with so many things such as you alone know or can know, most loving father. Yet I tore myself away and escaped from the ceaseless questions and petitions of everyone, and shut myself up alone with Nicholas, of whom you are so fond. There I refreshed myself again and again with the charm which emanated from your letter.[13]

The tone is close to that of a lover receiving a letter from his beloved, just as Aelred's lament over his dead friend Simon is reminiscent of a lover's cry of anguish at a physical loss:

Where have you gone, O example by whom I lived, O guide whom I followed? Where have you gone, where are you now? Where shall I turn? Whom shall I take for my guide? How are you torn from my embrace, rent from my kisses, hidden from my eyes? I will embrace you, dear brother; not with the flesh, but in the heart. I will kiss you, not with the touch of the lips, but with the affection of the mind.[14]

Our modern reaction to such language is to suppose that the sexuality which was not obtaining its normal outlet is overflowing here into the idea of friendship. It is hard to doubt that this was happening, but we must also remember that these images performed another function. The Song of Songs, in monastic tradition, expressed the ascent of the soul to God, and in using sexual symbolism derived from it the writers of the time were affirming that friendship was a primary means by which one might come into the presence of God.

The essence of friendship was a common mind, and that common mind was formed by participation in the love of Christ. This was the point of Bernard's appeal to raise ourselves above the daily practicalities of friendship into the love which was at its core:

> We wear ourselves out in scribbling to each other, and we exhaust our messengers in sending them backwards and forwards between us. But is the spirit ever weary with loving? Let us stop this tiring business of exchanging letters . . . Let us love and be loved; benefiting ourselves by loving, and others by being loved.[15]

It was among these Cistercian writers that the theme of the Christ-centredness of friendship was most fully developed. The imagery of paradise was applied at once to friendship and to the monastic life, and their understanding of both was deeply influenced by the language of the Song of Songs. Bernard's great series of sermons on this book, composed in the last two decades of his life, is only one, if the most impressive, example of the application of its symbolism. Aelred meditated on the "three kisses" as the road of ascent from the friendship of man to that of God.[16] He saw friendship, indeed, as the paradigm of the whole Christian life, and perhaps went further in its theory and practice than any other contemporary. Characteristically, however, he was careful to remain within the limits prescribed by tradition. At one moment in his dialogue he played with the dramatic proposition "God is friendship", but, although it plainly attracted him, he finally rested content with an adaptation of Cassian which went almost, but not quite, as far:

> IVO. But what does that mean? Are you saying of friendship what John, the friend of Jesus, said of charity: "God is Friendship"?
>
> AELRED. That admittedly is an unaccustomed phrase, and has no Biblical authority. But I certainly would not hesitate to apply to friendship what he goes on to say about charity: "He who dwells in friendship, dwells in God, and God in him."[17]

The experience of friendship was, properly understood, an encounter with God.

LOVE: THE TROUBADOURS

What the Church did for friendship, it signally failed to do for marriage. Although mystics and preachers were ready to employ the sexual imagery of the Song of Songs in expounding the union of God and the soul, they did not regard sexual experience itself as possessing any religious value. Their failure must be ascribed in part to existing social circumstances. For most people, marriage was not an uplifting experience. True, both history and literature tell us of happy marriages, but usually a marriage among the upper classes (about whom alone we are properly informed) was undertaken for political and social advantage, and was readily dissolved. Strictly, no doubt, the dissolution of a marriage was not recognized at the time. "Divorce", in our sense, was not legally possible. But the marriage law of the Church was in a state of extreme complexity, and was changing rapidly. There was doubt as to what precisely constituted a valid marriage, and an elaborate set of rules prohibited matrimony within a wide net of relationships. Those who wished to contract a valid marriage often found it necessary to engage in major litigation to clear themselves of possible barriers, and others preferred to marry in haste, preserving the convenient possibility of having the marriage broken subsequently. It is a remarkable fact that almost every English king between 1066 and 1216 found himself in a matrimonial–legal tangle of this sort, and England was in no way exceptional.* This was not an environment in which affection easily flourished. Nor was it encouraged by the Church. Although the upholders of the dominant ascetical tradition carefully guarded themselves from the condemnation of marriage as such, they regarded passionate love as essentially sinful, and were apt to quote the ungenerous

* William I and Henry I both had great difficulty in obtaining clearance from the Church for their proposed marriages. Henry II married a divorcee, Richard had major difficulties over his marriage contract with the French royal house, and John, having been once divorced, contracted a second marriage of dubious legality.

tag: "every ardent lover is an adulterer with his own wife" The Church offered little to lovers, even to those with honourable intentions.

As a result, the treatment of *amicitia* and *amor* by the writers of the time contrasted violently. The friendship-writers stood in a long Christian–classical tradition, on which they drew fully and freely, but there was no similar tradition to form and guide the discussion of sexual love. As far as our surviving evidence takes us, there was an enormous explosion of interest in the subject shortly before 1100. An almost complete silence was followed by the beginning of a love literature which challenged in quality and surpassed in volume that of any earlier civilization. The new love poets had no normative tradition to guide them. The learned could go back to Latin poetry, and most of all to Ovid; the less learned used sources (if they used them at all) which are no longer accessible to us. It is not surprising to find that there is a huge variety of attitudes to love: satire, obscenity, and fidelity all have their place. Most prominent of all was a new assumption, for which it is difficult to find earlier parallels: courtly love, which involved the service and adoration of the beloved, and which we must consider shortly in more detail. The sudden emergence of this ideal moved C. S. Lewis to a resounding declaration:

> The new thing itself, I do not pretend to explain. Real changes in human sentiment are very rare—there are perhaps three or four on record—but I believe that they occur, and that this is one of them.[18]

These splendid words require to be examined rather cautiously. They are, I think, true if they mean that no previous society had formulated courtly love as an ideal by which it lived. The twelfth-century knights increasingly came to see themselves as fighting for their lady's honour and renown. For many of them this became the accepted convention, for some a profound personal inspiration. Few warriors in previous societies had been similarly motivated, and it is fair to say that here we are in the presence of a huge change in the ideals of society, a change which made personal devotion the essential feature of a true man–woman relationship. In this sense, and it is a very important sense, Lewis was rightly underlining the beginning of a new chapter in Western culture. It is more difficult to follow him into some of the more detailed implications of his words. It seems to force the evidence if we say that the twelfth-century poets had *no* previous source from which they could draw their ideas. Ovid taught them at least the idea of seeking for the elegances and cultivated sentiments which may be found in love, and Lewis himself regarded "Ovid misunderstood" as a source of the courtly love convention. It would perhaps be fairer to speak of "Ovid adapted" as one of its guiding influences. It is even harder to accept the view, which seems implicit in his words, that we have here an actual change in human psychology, for parallels may be found in many places for the emotions which underlie courtly love, and notably for the desire to serve or adore the beloved.[19] These reservations, however, do not obscure the fact that we are in the presence of a new cultural pattern with great significance for the future.

The importance of this change, combined with its apparent suddenness, has led many scholars to seek for one specific point of origin. Attention has been focused on the troubadours, about whom Denis de Rougemont declared that "no one can doubt that the whole of European poetry issued from the poetry of the troubadours of the twelfth century".[20] Among the troubadours, Count William of Poitiers has been selected as the really creative mind, who first devised the concept of courtly love.[21] These views, which thus ascribe one of the major cultural features of the period to a private inspiration, rest on insecure foundations. One may agree readily with de Rougemont that the troubadours influenced a great deal of European vernacular poetry, but to say that such a literary form as the French or German romance "issued from" troubadour verse seems an indefensible statement. Similarly, it is true that Count William of Poitiers is the first troubadour whose poems we can identify, but this does not make him the only begetter of troubadour love poetry. He uses certain technical expressions which suggest that he was writing within a convention which already existed, and we know the name of a respected contemporary troubadour, Ebles of Ventadour, even if the latter's works do not identifiably survive. Even among the slim collection of Count William's remaining poems we find several styles: some amusing bawdry, a lament on his departure from Poitou, an obscure poem which may be satire or alternatively an early example of the later allusive and artificial style, and some courtly love poems. The reasonable conclusion is that the approaches to love characteristic of the troubadours were already established by about 1100 when Count William was writing.*

Strictly speaking, the origin of the courtly love convention is not a part of our present subject, but it is necessary to avoid any approach which gives too standardized a character to the discussion of love in the twelfth century by suggesting that it originated with one school or even with one writer.† The scene is extremely varied, even allowing for the elements of convention and common influences, and it is unfortunate that writers still quote on occasion the insensitive remark of a German critic, that all troubadour verse sounds as if it were written by the same poet.

Perhaps the safest way to picture what was happening is this. Already before 1100 there was a vernacular lyric poetry, now lost to us, which spoke of love among its other subjects, and which had influenced the composition of Latin lyrics.[22] In the late eleventh century, in various parts of Europe, the growing interest in love among upper-class society led to the emergence of more sophisticated erotic poetry. In Languedoc there was an aristocracy better educated than elsewhere,[23] eager for elegance, encouraged perhaps by a knowledge of the Latin lyric and by acquaintance with the cultivated society of Moorish Spain. Whatever the precise influences, the courts of Limoges and the south produced lyric poetry which was at once the first cultivated vernacular verse in

---

* It has sometimes been supposed that William's courtly love poems were his latest works, and that he "invented" the ideal in the course of his poetic career and subsequently gave up the composition of other types of verse. This chronology rests on no evidence whatever, and it is more natural to assume that he worked in various *genres*, most of which were subsequently represented in later troubadour verse. See the recent discussion by L. T. Topsfield, "The burlesque poetry of Guilhem IX of Aquitaine", *Neuphilologische Mitteilungen* 69, pp. 280–302.

† For a splendid satirical description of standardized courtly love, as it has been invented by modern scholars, see D. W. Robertson, "The Concept of Courtly Love as an Impediment to the Understanding of Medieval Texts", in *The Meaning of Courtly Love*, ed. F. X. Newman (Albany 1968).

western Europe, and an elaborate expression of admiration for the beloved in terms borrowed from feudal convention. In the north of France the same interest in love was manifested at much the same time, but the circumstances were different. Although lay courts and patronage were influential, vernacular culture was less developed and the love literature was in Latin. As a young monk, presumably before 1080, Guibert of Nogent, fired by a liking for Ovid and Virgil, composed poems about the elegances of love; so in varying ways did Marbod of Rennes probably, and Baudri of Bourgueil certainly. A little later Abelard was writing love songs which (as he remarked with characteristic modesty) remained popular and were sung in many districts; and in the 1130s we have the learned and passionate discussion of love in the correspondence between Abelard and Heloïse. When vernacular poetry developed in the north, it retained an element of classical and scholastic learning which was not so apparent among the troubadours. The early romances were based on stories of Greece or Rome, and many of the authors came to their work with a classical background: the earliest works of Chrétien de Troyes, for example, were adaptations of Ovid.

The troubadours were therefore one among several schools of writers who were discussing love, but they were a particularly interesting and influential group, and it will therefore help us to understand what was at issue if we concentrate our attention on one or two of them. It has already been mentioned that the earliest identifiable troubadour whose work survives was Count William of Poitou and Aquitaine, who died in 1127. Of the poets of the twelfth century one of the greatest was Bernard of Ventadour, whose work roughly covered the period 1145–75. Bernard was of low birth, the son of a castle servant; but, as Ventadour was already a great troubadour centre, his talents were recognized, and he started a career which won him honour in many courts, and took him as far afield as England, where Eleanor of Aquitaine, granddaughter of Count William, was queen. The troubadours wrote about many subjects, although Bernard himself was exclusively a love poet. The central theme of Languedoc love poetry was usually called *fin'amors*, or sometimes *verai'amors*. The nearest English translation is "true love", but as that phrase

carries more modern overtones it is perhaps best to accept the now
conventional rendering "courtly love". The spirit of *fin'amors* is
one of subservience to the beloved. The poet speaks of her in terms
of service, devotion, and, at times, of adoration. Fundamentally,
as we have seen, this attitude rests upon an aspect of human
psychology, but it was the peculiar contribution of Provençal
society to give this desire to serve an institutional expression, by
applying to it the language of feudal dependence. The lady may
be addressed inappropriately as *midons*, "my lord," and Count
William could already use the word "obedience" to mean the
amorous pursuit of ladies. The effect of this amalgamation of love
and feudal service was to make the "service of love" an accepted
attitude for a lover, to an extent it had probably never been before,
and it had the further effect of confining the troubadours within a
rather limited number of themes, centred on their obedience to
their chosen ladies. The context of troubadour poetry is the convention of the court, and, although they might complain of the
cruelty of particular ladies, the poets did not usually attack the
accepted code of manners. It was not in their interest to do so,
for they hoped that faithful service would be rewarded by either
love or money, and the lady was free to give or withhold, except
vis-à-vis her husband, who was not counted as a player in the game
of love. An exception to this general acquiescence was Marcabru,
who on occasion expressed himself mordantly about the whole
convention, to the annoyance of later poets, who probably felt
that their trade secrets were being laid bare:

Marcabru, son of Marcabrune,	*Marcabrus, fills Marcabruna*
Was born under a fickle moon	*fo engenratz en tal luna*
And knows that love will very soon	*qu'el sap d'Amor cum degruna,*
Grow dim.	*Escoutatz!*
For never did he other love,	*quez anc non amet neguna,*
Nor anybody else love him.[24]	*ni d'autra non fo amatz.*

It must be remembered that the troubadours were primarily song-
writers, interested less in the content of their verse than in the
music and the rich and complex rhymes which can be achieved in
Provençal. They are almost untranslatable, for their rhyme-
schemes cannot be reproduced in English, and the key-words
have often acquired more modern overtones.

The ideal of *fin'amors* was neither lofty nor profound. This is a poetry of desire, telling of the poet's joy or sorrow as he waits for his reward, but rarely celebrating the fact of fulfilment. Provençal love poetry thus has the air of being, like Oxford, the home of lost causes, and writers have jumped to the conclusion that the poets, amid their perpetual longing, did not desire physical intercourse with the beloved. Most of them, however, frankly said that they did; it was merely that they did not regard fulfilment as a subject for poetry. The love of which they spoke was a physical one, directed to the body of their lady and not to her beauties of character, which they rarely mentioned. The evidence supports the opinion that "*fin'amors* is a hidden love, adulterous and dominated by physical desire". It is distinguished from common-or-garden adultery by the requirement of sincerity and by certain conventions of elegance: "the ambition not to love like everybody else, like the general run of people. The sphere of courtly love is an ideal world, which is excluded from the comprehension and approach of the ignoble."[25] It was the self-indulgent ideal of an aristocratic milieu, and the troubadours' approach to love was confined within strict conventions and distorted by an odd social situation. We may readily admit that they were often not very perceptive about the human heart, and the *chansons de geste*, in spite of their limitations, often showed more insight into personal relations. They were in a position to make only a restricted contribution to the discovery of the individual.

Yet it would be wrong to stress exclusively the limitations and conventionality of the troubadours. They were capable, within these limitations, of distinctive and personal approaches to their central theme of love. We have already observed that Marcabru was capable of harsh satire. Jaufre Rudel's dedication of verses to his distant love, *amor de lonh*, gives his work a mark of its own, and Bernard of Ventadour goes far outside the conventional into the language of passion. It has been said that he "sang of love with the naïve passion of a primitive".[26] We know nothing of the lives of these men outside their poetry, and therefore are unable to say whether they had experienced what they described. It matters little. Whether autobiographical or not, Bernard's grand passion must have roused echoes in his hearers, or his works would not have been popular, as we know they were. Jaufre's *amor de lonh* gains rather than loses in significance if she is the product of his poetic imagination. For all their limitations these men were observers of the human heart in love, perhaps the first in the new Europe. The "distant love" theme placed the longing heart in a new, and revealing, light. The suggestion that Jaufre's love was for the Virgin Mary is very wide of the mark, as it is frankly physical, but it is a love which, for the moment, cannot find fulfilment, and which leaves the poet alone to reflect on his own emotions:

'Tis true that I am eager for,	*Ver ditz qui m'apela lechai*
That I desire, a distant love;	*Ni desiron d'amor de lonh.*
I place no other joy before	*Car nulhs autres jois tan no'm plai*
Enjoyment of a distant love.[27]	*Com jauzimens d'amor de lonh.*

Jaufre's situation, in an extreme form, is that of the troubadours generally. They await their reward. The service of the beloved gives them "joy", an unending theme in their poetry:

> Rejoicing, it is my desire
> In love, a life of joy to find;
> And since to joy I turn my mind,
> I must to greatest heights aspire.
> As fair a lady honours me,
> As you could hope to hear or see.[28]

> Mout jauzens me prenc en amar
> Un joy don plus mi vuelh aizir,
> E pus en joy vuelh revertir
> Ben dey, si puesc, al mielhs anar,
> Quar mielhs onra·m, estiers cujar
> Qu'om puesca vezer ni auzir.

The supreme poet of joy was Bernard of Ventadour, who had a remarkable skill in expressing the exhilaration of the lover and the sense that his joy spilled out into the world around:

> When grass grows green, and leaves appear,
> And blossom on the tree is gay;
> And nightingale aloud and clear
> Lifts up his voice and sings a lay;

He gives me joy; the flowers give me joy,
Joy in myself, and, in my lady, joy.[29]

Can l'erba fresch'e·lh folha par
e la flors boton' el verjan,
e·l rossinhols autet e clar
leva sa votz e mou so chan,
joi ai de lui, e joi ai de la flor
e joi de me e de midons major.

Yet this joy often gives way to sorrow, the sorrow of unsatisfied love:

The seasons come and go in varied play,
Days, months and years, in ever changing race.
But I, alas, do not know what to say,
For my desire is ever in one place.
It stands without remove,
For I have but one love,
And have not known the joy of her embrace.[30]

Lo temps vai e ven e vire
per jorns, per mes e per ans,
et eu, las! no·n sai que dire
c'ades es us mos talans.
ades es us e no·s muda
c'una·n volh e·n ai volguda
don anc non aic jauzimen.

The poet's personal happiness was thus bound up with his service of *fin'amors*, but he saw his love as carrying with it more than individual pleasure. Nature was the echo, or background, of love, and the troubadour felt himself sometimes in union, sometimes in discord, with the joyful colours of the southern spring. More profoundly, some poets discovered the meaning of themselves in their love. It was love which gave purpose to life, and Bernard could declare

That man is dead who has no sense
Of love's sweet savour in his heart.[31]

Ben es mortz qui d'amor no sen
al cor cal que dousa sabor.

This is the central theme of *Quan vei la laudeta mover*, which has
been acclaimed as one of the greatest of European lyrics:

Myself I cannot count as mine,
Nor could I, from the hour I saw
Within her eyes my image shine,
Clear in the mirror I adore.
Mirror, in my reflection there
I find deep sorrow lingering,
And I am lost, as was the fair
Narcissus, mirror'd in the spring.[32]

Anc non agui de mi poder
Ni no fui meus deslor en sai,
Que·m laisset en so solhs vezer
En un miralh que mout mi plai.
Miralhs, pos me mirei en te,
M'an mort li sospir de preon
Qu'aissi·m perdei com perdet se
Lo belhs Narcisus en la fon.

At much the same time Aelred was using this identical image of
the self mirrored in the beloved, but to very different purpose:
"The Cross of Christ is, as it were, the mirror of the Christian."[33]
Since Bernard discovers himself in the beloved, it is not surprising
to find that he goes further, and proclaims that love is the source
of all values:

Man without love is little worth;   *nuls om ses amor re no vau,*
And so I would not wish to have   *per qu'eu no volh, sia mia*
The ownership of all the earth   *del mon tota·lh senhoria*
Unless I could have joy as well.[34]   *si ja joi no·n sabi'aver.*

The note of grand passion is characteristic of this poet, and it is
interesting to hear the echo of Heloïse's declaration of love to
Abelard:

God knows that I never wanted anything from you, but you

yourself; desiring, not what was yours, but you alone. I did not look for the bonds of marriage nor any dowry, nor did I even consider my wishes and desires, but I endeavoured to satisfy yours, as you well know . . . I call God to witness that if Augustus, the governor of the whole world, offered me the honour of marriage and granted me the entire earth to be mine for ever, I would esteem it dearer and more noble to be called your prostitute than his empress.[35]

In declaring that *fin'amors* is the source of all that is valuable Bernard is in tune with many other troubadours. These values, of course, were those of their aristocratic society, the virtues of fidelity, joy, prowess, and courtesy (*cortezia*). Against the glorification of war as an end in itself, as in the poetry of Bertrand de Born, and against the cynicism of satirists, Bernard proclaimed, on behalf of the ladies and their troubadours, that true love is the foundation of all the courtly virtues. This idea was underlined at times by the use of religious and devotional language about the beloved, although this is much less prominent in troubadour verse than in that of some other schools of poetry.

There were, therefore, great differences between the ideals of *amicitia* and *fin'amors*, differences which reflect the contrast between the parts of society which favoured them. The cult of friendship was part of a broad understanding of reality, within which it was seen as one of the ways (sometimes, as the pre-eminent way) in which God revealed his presence to men. By contrast, courtly love was a brittle ideal, rooted in social convention but not connected with a wider vision of the world. Its practitioners were in the difficulty that they could neither reconcile their values with Christianity, nor suggest a viable alternative. The writers of northern France were actively aware of this dilemma, which they attempted to avoid in various ways; the troubadours of the south were less obviously troubled by it; but a certain brittleness in their way of life is perhaps indicated by the number of them who eventually became monks, especially Cistercians, a number which includes Bernard of Ventadour. The two ideals of friendship and love were expressed in ways essentially inimical to one another, and, in spite of the attempt of a few

literary men to champion both sets of values, they really belonged
to different ways of life.

It is all the more interesting to observe some real similarities.
Such resemblances, observed in contexts so diverse, can only be
understood as arising from assumptions held in common by most
men of the time. The first is the inclination to find in these personal
relationships the summit of human experience and the source of
good. As we have seen, these are common themes in both traditions. In detail the treatment of them differed greatly. The monk
hoped to find in friendship a common mind in Christ, while the
poet looked for love to inspire all the virtues of *cortezia*. One can
imagine in the mouth of a Cistercian the declaration that "man
without love is little worth", but it would have meant something
utterly different from what the troubadour intended. Yet there is
common ground here. Both systems rest on a desire to make
personal experience and personal relations the focus of life. Moreover, they do this in rather similar ways. Both are concerned with
self-analysis. Indeed, one doubts whether troubadour love can
really be regarded as an encounter with other people. The poets
showed little interest in their ladies' characters, and the more
sensitive writers were aware of the introspective nature of their
experience: when Bernard of Ventadour looked in his lady's eyes,
he saw himself. The twelfth century felt a persistent attraction
for the legend of Narcissus and the symbol of the mirror, which
were used to describe "the birth of self-consciousness through
love".[36] The same phenomenon may be observed among friendship writers. There are, indeed, exceptions; we have noticed the
insistence of Bernard of Clairvaux that one should love a friend
as he is. More often a writer is concerned with his own sensations
and sentiments, and the friend is an *amor de lonh*, whose true
character may be quite unknown to the other. We have here an
important qualification to what has been said in this chapter
about the contemporary interest in personal relationships, and it
applies almost equally to friendship and love. The element of
person-to-person encounter was less than one might suppose at
first sight, and the pursuit of love and friendship has to be regarded
as essentially an extension of that search for the self of which we
spoke in the previous chapter. The centre of interest was not the

friend or the mistress, but one's own self, the thoughts inspired, the passions aroused, by the distant beloved. Once possession was reached, the poetry was over.

The third point of similarity is closely connected with the second; but to understand it we must broaden our horizons, and compare the troubadour songs with a wide range of religious literature. Throughout this broad spectrum, the theme of longing, for what has not yet been possessed or realized, is prominent. We catch its echo in the *Dulcis Jesu memoria*, that splendid expression of Cistercian mysticism:

Desired with thousandfold desire,	*Desiderate millies,*
When wilt thou, Jesu, come to me?	*mi Iesu, quando venies?*
When wilt thou make me joyful, Lord?	*quando me laetum facies?*
When satisfy my heart with thee?	*me de te quando saties?*
Unending is the love of thee:	*Amor tuus continuus,*
My longing lasts, and does not cease;	*mihi languor assiduus,*
My sweetest Jesus is to me	*mihi Iesus mellifluus*
Unfailing fruit of endless peace.[37]	*fructus vitae perpetuus.*

Here, in the joy in the one so passionately desired (*desiderate millies*) and in the unsatisfied longing (*languor*), we are close to much troubadour verse. Nor is the expression of unfulfilled desire confined to the troubadours and Cistercians, for in subsequent chapters we shall observe it in the "quest" motif in the romances, and, very markedly, in the Jerusalem hymns. Etienne Gilson, in his study of Saint Bernard's mystical theology, included an interesting discussion of the prevalence of this theme of longing. He demonstrated convincingly, I think, that its presence in Provençal poetry is not the result of a direct religious influence, whether from Cistercian mysticism or from the cult of the Virgin. He pointed out that the expression of longing is an inevitable part of all love poetry, religious or secular; but this, while true in itself, does not account for its peculiar prominence in the literature of this time. Perhaps no single explanation can suffice for a feature so widespread, so much a part of the atmosphere. It must be linked with the assiduous attempt at self-understanding which we have now seen in so many forms. Men looked for a mirror in which they could see themselves clearly. The idea was a favourite one of theirs, and we have heard already how the sermon should reveal the hearers to themselves; how the lover sees his reflection in the lady; how Christ is the mirror of the Christian. It is reasonable to suppose that one thing, at least, which helped to produce this literature of longing, was the uncertainty about the nature and identity of the individual self. This uncertainty in turn was caused (or so it was suggested in the first three chapters) by changes which had robbed men of their certainty about their role within an evolving society and their confidence in their standing in an objective system of theology. The remaining chapters must be devoted to a further consideration of the effect of these changes upon the individual's image of himself.

6 The Individual and Society

Boiling over inwardly
With anger unconfined,
Now in deepest bitterness
I will speak my mind.
ARCHPOET

I will do as my heart wills
CHRÉTIEN DE TROYES

Primitive societies are usually conformist societies, not in the sense that a single code of behaviour is enforced upon their dissenting members, but in the more fundamental sense that their members are not aware of alternative patterns of conduct. The individual is instructed in the wisdom of the fathers, and expected to allow his mind to be shaped by the common mind of the tribe. There are few options open to him. The absolutely primitive society is perhaps a convenience of thought rather than an observable reality, for there must be few cultures which leave no elbow-room for human inventiveness, and which possess no powers of adjustment to changing circumstances. Certainly, western Europe about the year 1000 cannot be regarded as completely primitive, for its inheritance was a complex one, and the simple values of a military aristocracy were being challenged by other modes of behaviour, most notably that of the world-rejecting monastic orders.

Nevertheless, the contrast can still be validly made between the relatively primitive society of A.D. 1000 and the much more open one of 1150. The cultural, economic, and social changes of the intervening years had had the effect of creating for the individual a range of choice which was previously inconceivable. He could choose between various occupations: he might be a knight, a scholar, an administrator, or a monk. Moreover, within each of

these occupations, there was no clear or simple ethic. Men disputed as to the nature of true knighthood, and the polemic over
the proper form of the monastic life was furious. This awareness
of a conflict of values forced the individual to make his own
decisions, to question the conduct of those who presided over the
established order, and to seek a way of reconciliation which would
at once enable him to make his peace with other men and to be
true to himself. In one form or another, the problem of alienation
and order was central in the literature of the twelfth century,[1] and
the sense of alienation was expressed in one of the most powerful
symbols which have been devised for it: pilgrimage. This was
pre-eminently the age of the pilgrimage, and the Crusades were
envisaged very much in that light—indeed, there was until the mid-
thirteenth century no special word for a crusade, which was known
as *peregrinatio* or *expeditio*. In this chapter I shall consider two
reactions by the individual in face of society: the path of rejection
(as represented by the satirists) and of reconciliation (as represented by Chrétien de Troyes).

SATIRE

Satire does not, in itself, involve alienation. It does, of course,
indicate a conflict of *mores*, but it would be difficult to regard
Chaucer, for instance, as radically alienated, in spite of his genial
satire of the contemporary Church. Indeed, the satire of the later
Middle Ages had largely drifted into a static situation, in which
preachers and reformers repeated criticisms and jests worn smooth
with long usage, and no one expected much to happen; only
when satire was associated with peasant discontent do we feel the
breath of life in it. The twelfth century, however, was a different
case. It was the golden age of Latin medieval satire and the abuses
of the contemporary world were observed with a new clarity and
with cutting wit.

    This was the rebirth of satire, for there had been little of it
between the end of the classical world and the eleventh century,
and we may observe three reasons for its revival—reasons which
go far to explain the (to our eyes) strangely mixed character of
twelfth-century satire. The first of them is technical: the recovery

of *Latinitas*.² The men of the time knew their Juvenal and Horace, and still more significantly were thoroughly at ease with Latin as a literary medium. Their training in rhetoric helped them to construct a tirade against an opponent, and the modern reader is likely to be shocked by the virulence and apparent disregard for the truth shown in some polemical writings by men who were normally of honest and sober disposition. Invective was a mode of composition; a school-exercise which might be required for use on serious occasions, but which was governed by conventional rules of its own. This fact helps us to understand the merciless violence shown against his opponents by Bernard of Clairvaux; we are dealing here with a recognized mode of composition, which obeyed rules of art rather than the dictates of truth. One of the most scathing works of this kind, produced by a man with a high reputation for probity, was Gilbert Foliot's attack on Thomas Becket in his letter *Multiplicem*.³ He missed no rhetorical trick, as we may see from the sudden change of gear, from heroics to sinister suggestion, as he complained about Becket's abandonment of his colleagues and departure into exile:

> If battle is joined with the king, when we strike with the sword, we are open to the sword of retaliation; when we wound, we cannot avoid being wounded. Are your annual revenues so important to you that you want them to be earned by the blood of your brothers?

The cutting edge of the satirist's style, sharpened by a knowledge of the classics, was not the only new element in the situation. In the course of the eleventh century the tradition of monastic world-renunciation gave birth to a series of violent attacks upon the corruption of the Church.⁴ The emergence of satire was one of the signs that the monastic reformers had turned from a simple withdrawal from the world to a serious ambition to reform Church and society, and Peter Damiani was one of the earliest exponents of this idea in a series of pamphlets of remarkable pungency. This monastic origin left its mark upon the whole satirical tradition of the twelfth century, which was always ready to lapse into world-weariness, as in Bernard of Cluny's poem of about 1140:

The world is very evil;	*Hora novissima, tempora pessima*
The times are waxing late;	*sunt, vigilemus.*
Be sober and keep vigil,	*ecce minaciter imminet arbiter*
The Judge is at the gate.⁵	*ille supremus.*

This twofold ancestry, at once classical and monastic, gave a very distinctive character to the best satire of the time. Some of its writers were extremely witty men and highly adroit Latinists, but beneath this humanist surface they displayed a despair of the world and an expectation of its coming end. The voice is Jacob's voice, but the hands are the hands of Esau.

The third element in the development of satire was the managerial revolution which took place in the course of the twelfth century in both Church and State. The hope of the humanists had been that they would succeed in reforming the Church by obtaining the crucial positions within it, and that men of letters would govern the Church in place of the simoniacs and other corrupt clergy. It was not an idle ambition. At a time when, early in the century, Hildebert was bishop of Le Mans (and later archbishop of Tours); Marbod bishop of Rennes; Anselm archbishop of Canterbury; and Ivo bishop of Chartres; at such a time there appeared to be a real chance that humanists and monastic reformers would become predominant in the counsels of the Church. This hope was defeated in part by a technical development: the transfer of business into the hands of professional administrators, most of them lawyers. Older informal legal practice was replaced by procedures based on the Roman civil law, and the expert civilian or canonist became increasingly prominent in ecclesiastical administration. Already in 1150 Saint Bernard complained that at Rome more was heard of the law of Justinian than of the law of Christ,⁶ and later we hear the lament:

Now the pastor's seat is turned
Into a tribunal.⁷

The disappointment of the humanists was bitter. After the great development of literature, and the progress which had been made towards the reform of the Church, it now looked as if its last state would be worse than its first. To their opponents at least, the triumphant lawyers appeared as the agents of financial exaction, and the lawyers joined the court of Rome itself as the favourite targets for criticism. The growing legalism of the Church excluded from positions of influence and profit those whose skills were purely literary, and therefore created at the same time a target for criticism and a group of men admirably equipped for the composition of satire.

It would be a mistake to attempt to date these developments too precisely. The creation of a new class of administrators was inevitably a gradual process, but some indications can be given. The development of Bologna as a major centre for the study of canon and civil law took place in the years before 1140. In far-off England, the reign of Stephen (1135–54) was reckoned by several contemporaries as the time when the lawyers (*causidici*) came to England and when appeals to Rome began to flow. About 1150 we find the first uses of the word *officiales*, which in England* indicated the new legally trained class of episcopal advisers. Alexander III (1159–81) was the first pope to be an outstanding canonist in his own right. It would therefore be reasonable to say that in the decades after 1140 there was a marked tendency for the administration of the Church to fall into the hands of trained lawyers, and at the same time the training of the legal profession became increasingly technical. It became rare to find a man of wide educational sympathies who was also a good lawyer, as Ivo of Chartres had been, and John of Salisbury still was. It is in these years that we begin to discern a failure of nerve among the men of letters, as they realized that they were losing at once the power to influence policy in Church and State, and the hope of promotion for themselves. In England the Becket controversy played an important part in the process, for it involved the abandonment of the hopes which had until about 1159 been entertained of Henry II as a friend of the Church and of reform; a bitter division within the Church itself; the murder of the Archbishop in 1170; and, by way of final irony, the promotion within the English Church of those royal clerks who had most bitterly opposed Becket.

* It had been used earlier on the continent in a more general sense of servants or *ministri*, but even there its frequency increased enormously from about 1150.

This background of weakening humanist confidence helps to explain why, after the middle of the twelfth century, we find satirists who write as outsiders, as men who have lost hope in the cause of reform and confidence in their own prospects. Perhaps the finest among them was Walter of Châtillon, who wrote between about 1160 and 1190. Walter had been in the service of Henry II, but had left it, probably because of the dispute with Becket, over which he bitterly attacked Henry. Although a prominent man of letters, Walter had his own employment problems, and he showed a deep and personal hostility towards the new professional establishment in the Church. His account of the slimy members of the papal court is a masterpiece of satirical observation:

Sweetest songs they will produce,	*Dulci cantu blandiuntur*
And like Sirens introduce	*ut Sirenes et loquuntur*
Words intended to entrance.	*primo quedam dulcia:*
"*Frère, je te connais bien,*	"*Frare ben je te cognosco,*
And from you, *je ne prends rien,*	*certe nichil a te posco,*
For you come to us from France.	*nam tu es de Francia.*
"In your land you entertained us,	"*Terra vestra bene cepit*
And you handsomely retained us	*et benigne nos recepit*
When we needed a defence.	*in portu concilii.*
You belong to us (i.e.	*Nostri estis, nostri—cuius?*
To this apostolic see),	*sancrosancte sedis huius*
Children in a special sense."[8]	*speciales filii.*"

Walter's verse had much that is individual in both style and content, for he saw himself as a lone voice, defending values which were no longer esteemed. Beneath his scathing attacks on "Gratian's heirs" there lay a deeper sadness, a conviction that the time is out of joint, almost as if God did not care for man. In one of his poems he powerfully contrasted the order which, with the newborn confidence of rationality, men observed in the physical universe, with the disorder which prevailed among humanity:

God, who by a fourfold rule	*O qui quadrupliciter*
Chaos regulated,	*ylem figurari*
Things unequal equalized	*iubes, qui res dispares*
And by laws related,	*ita nexu pari*
All interrelationships	*comparas, ut nequeant*

1. Tomb-slab of
   Rudolf of Suabia
   (d. 1080)
   Merseburg Cathedral

2. Enamel plaque of
   Count Geoffrey of Anjou
   (d. 1151)
   Museum at Le Mans

4. Tombs of Henry II (d. 1189) and Eleanor of Aquitaine (d. 1204)
Abbey Church of Fontevrault

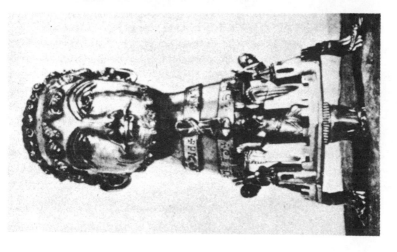

3. Head of Frederick Barbarossa
Made 1155/71. Cappenberg

Duly calculated—	*a se disparari;*
Why do you leave only man's	*cur permittis hominem*
Nature dislocated?	*sic denaturari?*

Since by principles secure	*Cum per certas methodos*
And Law's even reign	*et leges eternas*
You combine the elements,	*elementa copules*
Chaos to restrain,	*litemque discernas,*
Can it be that man himself	*videtur, quod hominem*
You alone disdain,	*solum modo spernas,*
And for his good government	*cuius vitam simili*
No concern retain?	*cura non gubernas.*

This poem is a particularly interesting example of the way in which the men of the twelfth-century Renaissance used the ideas of the past, but reshaped them to give them a new effect. The contrast of natural order and human anarchy comes straight from Boethius' *Consolation of Philosophy*,[10] and indeed was a commonplace of both the ancient and the contemporary world. But in Walter's hands it has gained a peculiar directness. The style, which in spite of its learned language remains simple and close to the vernacular, makes the verse a direct challenge to God, and it is significant that while for Boethius this sense of conflict was one which he transcended with the aid of Philosophy, for Walter it remains the truth about the world. The individual is calling God to answer for the imperfection of the world.

Walter could make sense of this situation in only one way: by eschatology. So gross a disruption of right order in the Church and society must indicate the coming of Antichrist and the approaching end of all things. It is at this point that we realize how much this thorough-going humanist had been influenced by the ideas of an earlier generation. He is confident, as Odo of Cluny had been, that he can see in the perversion of order the signs of the end. Walter apparently died a leper, an outsider in the cruellest sense. In one of his last poems he was, however, concerned, not with his personal misfortunes, but with the triumph of false values which heralded the end of the world. Its final, biting couplet was directed as ever against the careerists whose greed had destroyed the hopes of the humanists:

To a theme of sorrow	*Versa est in luctum*
Walter turns his lyre,	*cythara Waltheri,*
Not because excluded	*non quia se ductum*
From the clergy's choir,	*extra gregem cleri*
Nor does he complain	*vel eiectum doleat*
Because men disdain	*aut abiecti lugeat*
His unhappy state;	*vilitatem morbi,*
Rather does he fear	*sed quia considerat,*
That the world is near	*quod finis accelerat*
To its final fate . . .	*improvisus orbi . . .*
May this age's ending,	*Veniat in brevi,*
Year of Jubilee,	*Jesu bone Deus,*
Jesu, Lord and Master,	*finis huius aevi,*
Now come rapidly!	*annus iubileus!*
I would rather die than see	*moriar, ne videam*
Antichrist's ascendancy,	*Antichristi frameam,*
And his first advances	*cuius precessores*
Now within the Temple stand,	*iam non sani dogmatis*
There in an unholy band	*stant in monte crismatis*
Raking in finances.[11]	*censuum censores.*

One of the marks of the satire of the time, therefore, was its eschatology; men saw their enemies as figures in a last, terrible cosmic drama. Other writers moved in a different direction, and resorted to blasphemous parody. Such works as *The Gospel according to the Silver Mark* were exceedingly popular; it exists in many manuscripts and several different versions:

> The Lord Pope, hearing that his cardinals and ministers had received many gifts, was sick, nigh unto death. But the rich man sent him a couch of gold and silver, and immediately he was made whole. Then the Lord Pope called his cardinals and ministers to him and said to them: "Brethren, look, lest anyone deceive you with vain words. For I have given you an example: as I have grasped, so you grasp also."[12]

Even more scathing was a tract, dating from the beginning of the twelfth century, on the relics of the martyrs Albinus and Rufinus (i.e. silver and gold) describing their singular power in the court of Rome. The pamphlet culminated in a long speech by the pope which eventually became a great hymn of diabolical triumph:

In churches, in councils, in assemblies, in kingdoms, in cities,
in territories, in palaces, in towers, on land, on sea, everywhere,
we triumph, we reign, rule, entice, despoil, rape, betray, extort,
deceive, defraud and cheat.[13]

Perhaps the most popular of all the satirical poems of the century
was the anonymous *Apocalypse of Golias*, which probably owed its
widespread favour to the combination of two satirical genres,
eschatology and blasphemy. It is a parody of the Apocalypse
adapted to the circumstances of the contemporary church:

John wrote the visions he wondrously saw,	*Visa conscripserat ille mysteria,*
To the seven churches on Asia's shore.	*septem ecclesiis quae sunt in Asia:*
You, too, must write; but in different style,	*tu scribes etiam; forma sed alia,*
To the seven churches in England's fair isle.[14]	*septem ecclesiis quae sunt in Anglia.*

The "four living creatures, full of eyes" are interpreted as pope,
bishop, archdeacon, and dean, and the vision receives an interpretation of which the prophet did not dream:

Each of these creatures four wings on him bears,	*Ista sunt quatuor alas habentia,*
So he can fly on his business affairs;	*quia circumvolant rerum negotia:*
Each full of eyes, so that he can well see	*plena sunt oculis, eo quod praevia*
Profit at hand, and more profit to be.[15]	*lucra respiciunt, et subsequentia.*

The poem is filled with scarifying visions of the evils of the clergy,
and most of all of the monks, all of which were written indelibly
in the poet's brain by his angelic companion. Then, in the
splendid culmination of the poem, he is raised to the third heaven
to behold the very presence of God: and, in a witty conclusion
typical of so much of this satire, he admits that he had to eat the
bread of forgetfulness, and can remember nothing. All he is left
with is the bitter memory of a Church corrupted:

I fell from heaven like Cato before,	*De coelo cecidi ut Cato tertius,*
Nor can I tell you at all what I saw.	*nec summi venio secreti nuncius,*
But what my colleague upon me did write,	*sed meus mihi quod inscripsit socius.*
These things at least I can truly recite.	*hoc vobis dicere possum fidelius.*
O what a great and a marvellous story	*O quanta dicerem et quam mirifica,*
I could have told you of heavenly glory,	*de rebus superis et sorte coelica,*
Had not oblivion, brought by that bread,	*nisi papaveris coena sophistica*
Quite wiped the memory out of my head.[16]	*mentis vestigia fecisset lubrica.*

It will be evident that we are a long way from the naïve picture of
the Middle Ages as an age of faith. The nearest parallel to this
literature is perhaps to be found in the "sick verse" of our own
world. Its writers were men who had lost a clear sense of values,
or who had found their ideals betrayed by the very people who
ought to have defended them. They found obscene the spectacle
of the Church as a great propertied corporation and governmental machine, just as people in our day are revolted by the
sight of clergy blessing a nuclear submarine, and they were not
prepared to allow that the men of the establishment might at least
be sincere. The rebels were young men, who invented the drop-
out figure of the Goliard as the expression of their rebellion;[17]
the clerk without employment or prospects who lived only for
drink, gambling, women, and poetry. It is not clear how far the
satirists really were such men, or how far the Goliards adopted
this stance as a gesture of protest against their elders, whose
standards they rejected and whose pretensions they thought
hypocritical.

The greatest of the Goliardic writers was a poet whose name is
unknown to us, but whose nickname, the Archpoet, reflects his
standing among his admirers. He was a member of the household
of Rainald of Dassel, archbishop of Cologne and adviser of

Frederick Barbarossa, and his poems are mostly to be placed in the early 1160s. His "Confession" has, with the exception of a few hymns, become the best-known medieval Latin poem, and deservedly so. In form it is autobiographical, although it is less clear whether his life was as disorderly as he presented it. However this may be, it is a brilliant expression of the Goliardic view of life: on the surface, a gay and scintillating wit; and underneath, a boiling resentment directed against a society which found no place for their talents and offered no solution to the problems posed by a changing world. Helen Waddell has described this great poem as "the first cry from the House of the Potter, 'Why hast thou made me thus?' "[18] Not, indeed, that this was the only voice of protest. The Archpoet was the contemporary, perhaps the older contemporary, of Walter of Châtillon, and, different as they were in their character and opinions, they were similar in their bitter hostility to the whole order of things. The Archpoet's Confession stands as one of the greatest protests of the individual against a society whose standards he can neither accept nor fulfil.

Boiling over inwardly	*Estuans intrinsecus*
With anger unconfined,	*ira vehementi*
Now in deepest bitterness	*in amaritudine*
I will speak my mind.	*loquar meae menti:*
Of the lighter elements	*factus de materia*
Is my nature made;	*levis elementi*
I am like a leaf with which	*similis sum folio*
Gusts of wind have played.	*de quo ludunt venti.*

Usually we find that men	*Cum sit enim proprium*
Of wise disposition	*viro sapienti*
Like to sit their bottoms down	*supra petram ponere*
In a firm position.	*sedem fundamenti,*
I'm a fool, and much more like	*stultus ego comparor*
A fast-rushing torrent,	*fluvio labenti,*
For I find a stable life	*sub eodem aere*
Totally abhorrent.	*nunquam permanenti.*

I drift as a sailing-ship	*Feror ego veluti*
Would without a crew,	*sine nauta navis,*
As a bird is swept along	*ut per vias aeris*
Through the trackless blue.	*vaga fertur avis.*

Bonds can keep no hold on me,	*Non me tenent vincula,*
Nor can any fetter.	*non me tenet clavis,*
When I join my friends I get	*quero mihi similes,*
Worse instead of better . . .	*et adiungor pravis . . .*

I go down the primrose path	*Via lata gradior*
As most young men do;	*more iuventutis,*
Am addicted much to vice,	*implico me vitiis,*
Thoughtless of virtue.	*immemor virtutis,*
I am more for merriment	*voluptatis avidus*
Than renouncing sin,	*magis quam salutis,*
And, being dead in soul, I take	*mortuus in anima*
Good care of my skin.[19]	*curam gero cutis.*

The most individual of the protesters at this time provide an interesting study in the source of this sense of individuality. Partly, this is classical. They are classicists in their knowledge of the Roman poets and in their love of the Latin language, even though they did things with it which would have made Ovid blench. They are Christian in their knowledge of the Scriptures, from which indirectly they drew their sense of doom, the conviction that evil was no less than a cosmic disaster; and they are supremely adroit in misquoting Scripture to their own satirical ends—one is almost inclined to describe the Archpoet as a post-Christian writer. Certainly he did not learn that fierce awareness of himself in the pages of Horace, or even of Juvenal. Perhaps, however, the greatest debt of the satirists to Christianity was the contrast which worried the twelfth century as it does the twentieth: the gap between the poor man of Nazareth (of whose humanity men were keenly aware) and the elaborate machinery of the Church. Satirists were compelled to protest against this terrible distortion of an ideal, without, as a rule, having much idea how to remedy the situation. This is certainly the tension which lies behind the works of Walter of Châtillon, and possibly, although there the case is more complicated, behind the Archpoet. The problem was posed with such admirable clarity by a writer of a later generation that, even though he wrote in the thirteenth century, it seems appropriate to end with his comment on the situation:

Then Charity spoke out:
"O man, why do you doubt?
Why do you trouble me?
I am not there to see
In Orient or Occident,
In royal court or baron's tent
In cloister, or in papal writ;
Nor with the judges do I sit.
But down from Jericho I ride,
And with the wounded man will stay,
From whom the Levite turned away,
And passed by on the other side."[20]

Respondit Caritas;
homo, quid dubitas,
quid me sollicitas?
non sum quod usitas
nec in euro nec in austro,
nec in foro nec in claustro,
nec in bysso nec in cuculla,
nec in bello nec in bulla.
de Iericho sum veniens,
ploro cum sauciato,
quem duplex Levi transiens
non astitit grabato.

CHRÉTIEN DE TROYES

A poet of a quite different kind who was concerned with the relationship between the individual and society was Chrétien de Troyes. A contemporary of Walter of Châtillon, he was presumably a native of Troyes in Champagne, and his literary career probably extended from about 1165 to 1190. His works suggest a good education, probably in a cathedral school. He knew his Ovid, had a delicate taste in satire, could sustain an argument throughout a long romance, and was addicted to elaborate imagery. In training and outlook he was therefore substantially different from the majority of troubadours. Nevertheless, Chrétien, like them, wrote for upper-class lay society. He worked for Countess Marie of Champagne, the daughter of Eleanor of Aquitaine, and subsequently for Count Philip of Flanders. His assumptions were intensely aristocratic. His stories were all set among the nobly born, and on the rare occasions when a character of obscure origins, such as Perceval in *The Story of the Grail*, showed himself capable of noble actions, it turned out that he was well born without being aware of it. His themes were the aristocratic ones of chivalry and love, told within the framework of the much admired "matter of Britain", or Arthurian legends. The starting-point of most of his romances is the alienation of the hero from the society around him, and this is caused by a failure, or apparent failure, in either prowess or love. This is particularly clear in *Erec and Enide*. Erec's fault was to abandon the pursuit of arms in order to spend too long with his wife Enide: "All the knights said it was a great pity and misfortune that such a valiant knight as he used to be should no longer wish to bear arms."[21] This was "the reproach that made him set out".[22] The drama of the story, which is sustained among many battles and adventures, lies in the reconciliation of the hero with those who have rejected him.

This may make Chrétien sound like a society poet *par excellence*, for whom the final good was conformity to the values of the court. He has, indeed, often been seen in this light, but to represent him in this way is to misunderstand the character of the society for which he was writing. It did not possess a clear code of behaviour in matters of prowess and love, and to judge by the works of Chrétien and other writers of romances, their audience dearly loved a good argument about what was proper behaviour. Should a knight who had vanquished an opponent release him or kill him? How should a true lover balance the conflicting claims of prowess and devotion? The attention which Chrétien devoted to such questions suggests that he expected his hearers to enjoy their discussion. Sometimes he has the air of giving them a lesson, as when Perceval's mother expounds the nature of true chivalry, and at times Chrétien even explains some quite elementary point of good manners. His most interesting statement of an ethical position, however, is to be found in his handling of the ideal of married love. In both *Erec and Enide* and *The Knight of the Lion* (or *Yvain*) he presents as the true goal a life in which prowess and love are balanced, and love is to be found within marriage. Here he diverged sharply from such a poet as Bernard of Ventadour, who believed that prowess derived its value from love, and that love was achieved in despite of jealous husbands. Chrétien, in these two romances, has a reasonable claim to be the first exponent* of romantic love, and of "marrying for love", in the sense in which these have been understood by later European tradition. They are certainly stories with a moral, but it is not easy to be sure whether Chrétien was working out an idea for dramatic purposes, or whether he was recommending a code of living to his hearers. The

* But the author of *Ruodlieb* in Germany about 1050 was already showing an interest in such a theme, and perhaps deprives Chrétien of his claim to complete originality.

difficulty about the latter view is the fact that in *The Knight of the Cart* (or *Lancelot*) he contradicted the ideals of the other stories. It is the famous story of the adulterous love of Lancelot and Guinevere, and in it love is presented as the sole purpose of life, for which Lancelot is prepared to endure any humiliation. It may be that Chrétien, as a great artist, was prepared to work out an idea that had undoubted dramatic force. It is also possible that he wrote *The Knight of the Cart* under protest, instructed to do so by his patroness. It is certainly true that he left it unfinished and subsequently moved to another patron, and several passages suggest that he regarded Lancelot with a satirical eye. The scene in which Lancelot alternately fought valiantly and ran away ignominiously, according to his mistress's instructions, presents him as a figure of fun, and it may well be that Chrétien intended his audience to feel distaste at Lancelot's genuflexion to the bed on which he had committed adultery. For our purpose, however, it is not a matter of the first importance whether Chrétien changed his ethical position according to his artistic needs, or whether he was personally committed to the ideal of love within marriage. The significant thing is that ethical assumptions varied in the society for which he was writing, and that it expected, and enjoyed, the discussion of conflicting codes of conduct. There was agreement that chivalry and love were the great things in life, but no common set of rules for playing these two absorbing games.

It was inevitable, therefore, that Chrétien should be concerned with questions of individual behaviour, and of the character which lay behind it. It is informative to observe how far this courtly writer went in his interest in the individual. Firstly, Chrétien shared the concern with psychology which we have already seen to be a feature of his age. He took great pleasure in describing, not only external actions, but also the thoughts and emotions of his characters.* He was clearly fascinated by the differing qualities of peoples' minds, and especially by their varied attitudes to love. We may, for instance, contrast a description of a shy, golden first

---

* For Chrétien's interest in interior monologue, and his indifference to realism, see E. Vinaver, *The Rise of Romance* (Oxford 1971), esp. ch. ii. This way of thinking is argued there to have been founded on the concepts involved in the teaching of grammar in the medieval schools.

love (Soredamors) with the obsessive, adulterous passion which devoured Lancelot, to the point that he could forget what he was doing or even who he was. Chrétien also was adept at the expression of character through word and action, as in the mordant and graceless speeches of Keu. It must be said, indeed, that by the standards of a later age there is a grave failure to carry through a consistent observation of character, and that we are dealing with a series of set-pieces and vivid sketches, which can be found side by side with passages which lack any sense of character. *The Knight of the Lion* has often been admired, with justice, for the delicate and witty account of the heroine's rapid change from hatred of Yvain, who has killed her husband in battle, to a passionate love for him. At the end of the same story, however, the plot is resolved by an external device—Yvain and Laudine are reconciled by the wording of an ambiguous oath, and almost no account is given of their inner feelings about it. While, therefore, Chrétien at his best is capable of skilful type-characterization, there are strict limits to his interest in it. No one would suggest that he approached the depiction of individuals in the manner of Shakespeare, but even the characters which he does present are not continuously maintained. We have the same impression as in our study of the early portrait; a keen sense of human personality struggles for expression within an art form not yet adapted for the purpose.

A second sign of individualism is in the stress laid on the voluntary actions of the heroes. They normally set off on their quest for adventure against the resistance of those around them, and their impelling motive is not conformity to requirements, but the desire for a personal excellence far beyond normal expectation. As the hero approaches his greatest test, the deliberate and free nature of the choice is underlined. Erec persisted in his supreme adventure, the *Joie de la Cort*, in spite of being expressly told that "it is something from which you are free to change your mind and withdraw, if you will consider your own good".[23] Similarly with Yvain at the Castle of *Pesme Avanture*: "My foolish heart draws me there; I will do as my heart wills."[24] In the affairs of love, too, Chrétien is aware of the way in which the power of the heart surpasses the expectations of custom, as between Laudine and Yvain:

"I never heard of such a thing as this: that you put yourself
freely and absolutely in my power, without anyone's forcing
you . . ."
"Lady", he says, "the force comes from my heart, which is
attracted towards you. My heart has fixed me in this desire."[25]

This theme of following one's heart appears to be crucial to
Chrétien's ethics, in so far as these can be deduced from his stories,
and it is clearly an individualist rather than a conformist idea.
Chrétien was also aware that alienation from society is not a
simple situation, and that it rouses echoes within the experience
of the individual, influencing his most intimate relations with
others. Erec, as we saw, was driven on his quest by his discovery
that he was being called "recreant" for his neglect of chivalry.
However, this is not a simple case of the rejection of an individual
by society. It was Enide, his wife, who inadvertently told Erec
of the criticisms which were being made, and he took her with him
on his travels. There were, therefore, three elements woven into
the story: the rehabilitation of Erec's reputation in society, the
proof to Enide that he was as brave as ever, and the testing of
Enide to see if she still loved him faithfully. The story ends with
the two lovers reconciled, and with Erec restored to his place of
honour at Arthur's court and in his own kingdom; the individual
has found himself by finding his proper role in chivalry and love.
    Recent study has been particularly directed to the clarification
of Chrétien's symbolism.[26] Such an approach has its hazards, but
it is encouraged by the prominence which he himself gave to his
use of symbols—it is no accident that the later romances take their
title, not from the hero's name, but from the central image: *The
Knight of the Cart*, *The Knight of the Lion*, and *The Story of the
Grail*. While the interpretation has varied greatly, this line of
study has tended to stress the central significance for Chrétien of
the hero's search for his true self. One example of this is the use
of the name. Some of the heroes have curious periods of anony-
mity. Thus, at the beginning of *The Story of the Grail*, the
young man's mother underlines the importance of names: "Never
on the way or in hostel, have a companion long without asking
him his name; know the name of the person, for by the name one

knows the man."[27] Yet the young man himself has no name, and to the inquiries of a party of knights he can only say that he is called "Fair Son", "Fair Brother", or "Fair Lord". Once he has seen the Grail, he is able to *guess* that his name is Perceval, although he still does not know. Later still, after a strange and haunting episode in which he meditates on three drops of blood in the snow, he is able to say without hesitation that he is Perceval. The detailed interpretation of this is obscure, but it is hard to avoid the general conclusion that Perceval is engaged in discovering his true self ("for by the name one knows the man") and that this self-discovery has some connection with his deepening understanding of what it means to be a knight. Another type of imagery which points in the same direction is the use of "double" or "parallel" characters. A striking case is in *Erec and Enide*. Erec had been reconciled with his wife, and the story, in a real sense, had come to an end. But then Erec voluntarily, as is heavily stressed, undertook the great adventure of *Joie de la Cort*. This involved him in vanquishing Mabonagrain, who lived in an enchanted garden, apart from the world, in total amorous subjection to his lady. The impression is inescapable that this is what we would call Erec's false self, the Erec who dallied all day with Enide, and that Erec's greatest triumph is the victory which liberates his true self.

In this chapter I have considered two forms of literature which were concerned with the nature of social ideals: satire, which existed to comment on those ideals, and the romance, which expressed the outlook of the courts. Both were affected by the individualism of the period, but in different ways. At its sharpest satire served to record the protest of the individual against a society which he found intolerable. In the hands of Chrétien the romance told of the hero's discovery of his true self, a self which must live in reconciliation with society, but by no means in subservience to it.

7 The Individual and his Religion

My secret is mine; my secret is mine
BERNARD OF CLAIRVAUX, quoting from Vulgate

Throughout its history, the Church has seen itself as living between two fixed points: between God's saving act in Christ, and the completion of that salvation at the end of the world. The interpretation given to these events, whether past or future, has always had a corporate and an individual aspect; they have been thought of as significant for each believer, but also for the Church and the world as a whole. It would be naïve to divide the history of the Church into two ages, that of the "corporate" and that of the "individual". Yet it is true that if we turn to the writings of the Fathers we are usually struck by the objective social content given to the Cross and the Last Day. Much more than in the theology with which we are familiar the weight fell upon the assertion that God's action has changed, or will change, the status of humanity; while its importance for each believer, although not ignored, was usually given a subsidiary place. A marked change in this interpretation can be discerned with the emergence, during the period 1050–1200, of medieval or scholastic theology.

THE PASSION

With regard to the first of these two points of reference, the passion, the stress during the first thousand years fell upon the victory which God had won in the cross, a victory which overcame the devil's hold upon men, opened all mankind to the action of God's grace, and established Christ's lordship over the world:

Death and life have contended
In that combat stupendous:
The Prince of Life, who died, reigns immortal.[1]

A later age thought more readily of other things: the nature of Christ's sufferings, the love which he showed in them, and the pains he endured for the sinner's redemption. While one could not say that such thoughts were wholly foreign to the early Church, they played little part in comparison with the vision of the cross as a divine victory. Even during the Carolingian period, when there was a tendency in some writers to insist on the details of the sufferings which the Lord endured,[2] the element of objective thanksgiving remained predominant. The movement towards a more inward and compassionate devotion, in which the individual strove imaginatively to share in the pain of his Lord, became really strong in the eleventh century, and in the twelfth it governed much of the thought about the passion.

An early and important manifestation of the new spirit was a change in the form of the crucifix. Instead of the former figure of the living Christ, sometimes radiant with vitality, we find Christ dead on the cross. The first surviving example is probably the great wooden cross made for Archbishop Gero of Cologne (969–76), which is a moving study of majesty in death.* The head is slumped on the right shoulder, the eyes closed, the face twisted, the jaw hanging open. Between 1000 and 1200 artists working within this tradition strove to combine in their sculpture the agony and the majesty of Christ. The fact of death was clearly shown, and the attitudes of the watchers, Mary and John, became much more expressive of personal grief. On the other hand, the wounds of Christ did not receive anything like the exaggerated treatment which became usual later in the Middle Ages, the crown of thorns was rarely shown, and a kingly crown often appeared on Christ's head. The best works combined the glory and the suffering into a moving portrait of the dying King of Love. A fine example of this treatment is the crucifix on the casket of the Three Kings made by Nicholas of Verdun for Cologne about 1200.†

The change in the appearance of the crucifix corresponded with a growing devotional emphasis on the pains of Christ, which can be observed in the eleventh century, especially among the monastic reformers, whose contribution to the growth of a more inward,

* Plate 6.   † Plate 8.

and less formal, spirit we have already noticed. One way of illustrating this change is to compare a Carolingian work and a twelfth-century one: the *Short Treatise on the Passion of the Lord*[3] by Candidus Bruno (*c.* 825) and the meditation on the passion in the *Rule for Contemplatives* (*de Institutione Inclusarum*) by Aelred of Rievaulx[4] (*c.* 1150). With an interval of three centuries, we should expect large differences; but the purpose of the two meditations is broadly similar, and it is instructive to see in what ways the new spirituality has diverged from the old. The structure of the works is alike in that each follows step by step the events of the passion, or, in Aelred's case, of Christ's life as a whole. We are at once struck by the much more practised air of Aelred's treatment; whereas Candidus moves jerkily from text to text, the meditation of Aelred flows with an ease which indicates, not only literary excellence, but long experience of a flexible mode of meditation. The substance, too, is different. The ninth-century author does not dwell at length on the sufferings of Christ, but is interested rather in interpreting the story symbolically. Some of his comments are bound to appear to us, in the context of a crucifixion, strangely cold-blooded: "The crown of thorns placed on the head of Christ can also signify the sin of idolatry, by which the peoples ignorant of his true divinity imposed the divine name on various figments of idols."[5] It is consonant with this treatment that Candidus shows distinct reservations about the humanity of Christ: "The Lord, being made man, allowed into himself human affections when he willed, and used them as he willed. He said he was thirsty, and he said true: therefore he thirsted when he willed, and as much as he willed."[6] Aelred's spirit is very different. We find a new stress on compassionate participation in the Lord's passion. The only visual aid which Aelred would allow for use on an altar was "an image of the Saviour hanging on the cross, which will represent to you his passion, which you are imitating".[7] The importance of the individual's suffering with Christ is now paramount: "I know that pity now fills your heart, anguish inflames your inward parts. Allow him to suffer, I beg, for he suffers for you." There are no reservations about the humanity of Jesus—on the contrary, it was the divinity which was veiled: "Why so, my God? So filled with compassion for me you show yourself a man, and almost seem to be unaware that you are God."[8]

This deep personal bond with the crucified Saviour was characteristic of Aelred. On his death-bed, when no longer able to speak, he still wept at the Lord's suffering, and smiled at his love, as the passion story was read to him, and he recovered his voice to make a last act of hope while his friend Walter Daniel held a crucifix before his eyes.[9] In all this he was at one with his generation, and we can observe the growth of a variety of practices which reflect devotion to the crucified Jesus and a more intimate sense of personal commitment. The elevation of the host, which first appeared in the Mass in the early twelfth century, was interpreted as a reminder of the crucified humanity, and probably derived its popular appeal from that. The Crusades owed much of their support to this spirit—Bernard of Clairvaux' treatise *In Praise of the New Militia* was at once a handbook of crusading theory and a meditation on the holy places where Jesus lived and died. A new position of prayer was widely adopted, which subsequently became conventional; kneeling with the hands together. It was the position of homage, and its use expressed the personal loyalty which the believer felt for his Lord. Its general popularity was the work of the Franciscans, but it is highly probable that this rather startling transformation of a feudal ceremony into a devotional attitude had already taken place in the twelfth century.

An extreme representative of this tendency towards personal and individual commitment was Peter Abelard, who adopted this attitude so radically that he produced hymns that might have been written in 1400, and an atonement theory much admired by the liberals of 1900. The language of passion hymns generally remained traditional until the thirteenth century. The main occasion for such hymns was not, as we should expect, Lent and Good Friday, but Holy Cross day. There was something of a change in style in the twelfth century, the imagery becoming more complex, but they retained the objective and triumphant tone of the hymns from Carolingian and earlier days. To this there is a striking exception in the hymn-book composed by Abelard, some time between 1128 and 1140, for the convent of the Holy Paraclete, where Heloïse was abbess. When we open its pages, a new and strident note strikes us like a blow in the face.[10]

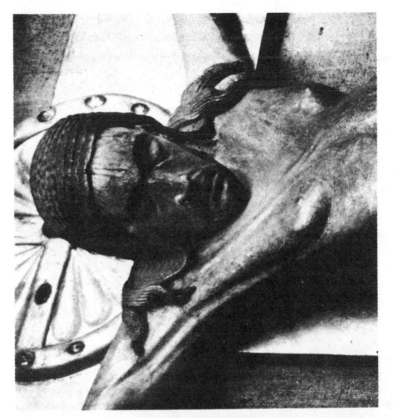

6. Gero Cross. Late tenth century
Cologne Cathedral

5. Crucifixion from façade of abbey of Saint-Mesme
Tenth century. Museum at Chinon

8. Crucifixion, Three Kings Casket
About 1200. Cologne

7. Crucifixion Scene from Codex Egberti
Late tenth century. Trier

For they are ours, O Lord, our deeds, our deeds; *Nostra sunt, Domine, nostra sunt crimina:*
Why must thou suffer torture for our sin? *quid tua criminum facis supplicia?*
Let our hearts suffer for thy passion, Lord, *quibus sic compati fac nostra pectora,*
That sheer compassion may thy mercy win. *ut vel compassio digna sit venia.*

The hymns provided for Good Friday and Holy Saturday were based on a new principle in hymnography, each resting in turn on one of the events of the passion, and each ending with the same verse:

So make us have compassion on thee, Lord, *Tu tibi compati sic fac nos, Domine,*
That we may sharers of thy glory be: *tuae participes ut simus gloriae;*
Heavy with weeping may the three days pass, *sic praesens triduum in luctu ducere,*
To win the laughter of thine Easter Day. *ut risum tribuas paschalis gratiae.*

The stress on compassion here is enormous. It becomes almost the central point of the passion, as if man was justified by compassion, by pity for suffering humanity.

The full force of this is apparent when we turn to Abelard's atonement doctrine. Abelard was not alone in being uneasy about traditional ideas of the atonement. Like him Anselm had impatiently rejected the view that the devil had rights over man, which were abolished through Christ's victory. Anselm, however, had constructed an "objective" theory of another kind. He accepted that in Christ God had altered the relationship between himself and mankind, quite apart from whether a given individual entered into that new relationship. Although his account of God's act differed greatly from that of previous thinkers, he was at one with them in this important respect. Abelard's theory, however, was a wholly "subjective" one. The cross had no meaning for him apart from the individual's response to it in love and compassion. In this he went so much further than his contemporaries that some scholars have argued that his subjectivity was not absolute, and indeed one must admit that some traditional language does linger in his writings and that his fullest discussion of the atonement unfortunately does not survive. Yet it is difficult to evade the force of such a passage as the following:

> It seems to us that *this* is the way in which we have been justi-fied in the blood of Christ, and reconciled to God: that by this singular favour shown to us (that his Son took our nature, and persevered until death, providing us with both teaching and example) he bound us more fully to himself by love . . . And so our redemption is that great love awoken in us by the passion of Christ, which not only frees us from the slavery of sin, but acquires for us the true liberty of the sons of God, that we may fulfil all things more by love of him than by fear.[11]

The same note was struck by a pupil of Abelard in a pregnant phrase: "those who live in him—that is, imitate his life".[12] Individualism could hardly go much further. The first passage reduces the traditional language about ransom and sacrifice to the believer's gratitude for the love of God shown in the cross. The second applies the same treatment to the concept of "life in Christ", which is glossed as meaning, not the totality of the sacramental life of the Church, but the believer's imitation of the Master. In all this the school of Abelard was not wholly out of touch with contemporaries—rather, they took contemporary individualism to an extreme, and thus anticipated similarly radical movements in the modern world.

ESCHATOLOGY

The salvation which had been offered, or achieved, in the death and resurrection of Christ still awaited its fulfilment. The expecta-tion of the final end (or eschatology) in the Western Church was substantially that formulated by Saint Augustine. God had appointed an end to the course of human history, when the dead would be raised, to receive their final reward. The Last Day was to be the culmination for humanity as a whole and therefore also for the individuals who composed it. No clear view had been formulated about the departed saints, but it was usually supposed that they were "asleep with Christ", awaiting their reward in the resurrection of their bodies. The general resurrection at the Last Day was therefore the hope of humanity in general and of each man in particular. It was accepted that the end would be preceded by a time of troubles, and by the coming of Antichrist, but that the date of this was not known. As one would expect, writers such as Odo of Cluny and Walter of Châtillon, who saw their own age as a time of troubles, were disposed to expect Antichrist's arrival in their lifetimes. Others uttered warnings against prophecies which would alarm the masses without foundation, and one must remember that, as at all times in the Church's history, the use of eschatological language might be intended, not as a prediction, but as a call to action—when Saint Bernard described in turn the anti-pope Anacletus, and Peter Abelard, as Antichrist, he was demanding that the Church should decide against them, and probably did not mean that the end of the world had arrived.

Like so many accepted opinions the traditional eschatology was challenged and transformed during our period. It was under pressure from two directions: from millenarian expectations, and from what we may call "spiritualism". Millenarianism does not directly concern our subject, but it is necessary to mention it briefly as a background to what was happening. Its essential characteristic was the expectation of a golden age upon earth, in which the saints would "come to life again, and reign with Christ a thousand years" (Rev. 20.4). It came in many shades, but in two principal colours. A conservative version was the belief that, before the coming of Antichrist, there would be a reign of peace in which the last Emperor would govern the whole earth. This idea had entered the West in the mid-tenth century, in the writings of Abbot Adso of Montier, and the French and German monarchies both showed themselves alive to the political advantages of encouraging the legend. It was conservative in the sense that it looked for no transformation of the existing order, but rather for its extension and completion. Other millenarian movements, however, were much more revolutionary. Preachers and agitators looked for the reign of the righteous poor, emphasizing the "righteous" or the "poor" according to whether their main interest was the transformation of the Church, or the overthrow of the social order. Such expectations were found among the poverty and preaching movements of northern France and in the popular Crusades, and they culminated in the thirteenth century in the views of the Spiritual Franciscans. Apart from one or two flirtations the official Church would have nothing to do with the more radical millenarian expectations, which always remained at, or beyond, the fringe of the Catholic body.

At the same time as it was being attacked from without, the traditional eschatology was being spiritualized from within by orthodox writers. It is not easy to give a cut-and-dried description of this process, for the existing doctrine was not being consciously modified; rather, it was being drained of much of its life, while the original vitality flowed into the relationship between God and the individual. Henri de Lubac has expressed what was happening in these words:

> The collective eschatology and the expectation of the final resurrection, whose outline was once so clear, are fading away. Within a framework which is still in general that of the church, the attention of the faithful is fixed less on the destiny of the church than on the destiny of each believer.[13]

One sign of this process was the development of individual meditation, in the same way as men were learning to reflect personally on the passion. The "four Last Things", which later became so conventional and popular a formula, appears in the *Sentences* of Peter Lombard in the middle of the century. It was, of course, not supposed that the Last Judgement had no objective reality, but the weight was now being placed on the answer which the individual must make. Another development pointed in the same direction. The Fathers, as has already been mentioned, were content to be ambiguous about the status of the departed. Sometimes they spoke as if the saints know what happens on earth, and as if the rank and file of the faithful are undergoing preparation for their final perfection. At other times the emphasis lay on the sleep which the departed enjoyed with Christ: "Give them rest where the light of thy countenance visiteth." This ambiguity was now replaced by a full-blooded conviction that the saints are already receiving their reward, and the imperfect their purgation.

In this new scheme the decisive moment is the death of the individual. The final resurrection of the body was in no way denied, but its importance had become peripheral and remote—a startling development, when one considers that the resurrection was at first the characteristic message of Christianity. The "three-fold body" of the Church, a favourite formula with writers in our period, was modified in the course of the twelfth century, its third clause (the bodies in the tomb, awaiting resurrection) being replaced by a new one (the Church expectant in purgatory). The saints were now unambiguously proclaimed as "the souls which reign with Christ in heaven".[14] The significance of the change is apparent in the last chapter of Peter Damiani's *Institutio Monialis*:

> The spirit is lifted up to the things which are promised in the homeland, that the exile may take little account of the harshness of the way. . . Recollect therefore how happy he is who, when so great a multitude of the unworthy is rejected, deserves to enter the marriage feast, amid the shining ranks of the elect; what an honour it will be to stand always before the eyes of the Creator, to contemplate the form of Truth in His very presence; to see God face to face, to be among the angelic choirs.[15]

Earlier eschatology had kept a balance, or alternatively a tension, between an individual and a corporate expectation. The particular person might look forward to his own release, but he did not normally count upon the perfection of his happiness until the renewal of the creation and its final perfection in the general resurrection. Imaginatively, the whole strength of eschatology now became attached to the individual. The Last Judgement was not denied (to suggest that for the Middle Ages would be absurd), but attention was concentrated upon one's personal answer and personal hope of heaven—if necessary, after a stay in purgatory. The world of Damiani is the world of *The Dream of Gerontius*. The uneasy combination of private and corporate hopes had now been resolved into the individual's desire for heaven. True, as we have already seen, some writers of unquestioned orthodoxy were actively concerned about the end of the existing order. Walter of Châtillon expected the coming of Antichrist because of the corruption which was evident in the life of the Church, and Otto of Freising saw in the progressive movement of learning from East to West the sign of the approaching end.* Most of those who entertained expectations of the collapse of the world order did so without any assumption that it would be succeeded by another, and better, society in this world; they were not, as a whole, millenarians. They therefore did not present a real contrast to the general tendency to individualize expectations of the future life. The interest of the Cistercians was concentrated on the encounter of God with the human soul, and the writings of William of Saint Thierry are not centred round any general eschatological expectation. These writers were working within a framework of traditional spirituality, but they developed the elements of individualism within it and made little use of other parts of the received teaching. Hildebert of Lavardin and Abelard had moved further from tradition. Although they would not for one moment have denied the idea of a Last Judgement, for them the heart of the matter lay in the deliverance of the believer from sorrow and sin—a view which tallied well with the intense individualism of Abelard's doctrine of the atonement.

A total assessment of the conception of the Last Things at this time would require a book in itself, and is not germane to our present purpose. The point made here is a more limited one: that in a number of circles the destiny of the individual was becoming the centre of attention, and the theme of the renewal of all things was slipping into a secondary place. This process is illustrated by the Jerusalem literature at this time. Jerusalem had always been a favourite Christian symbol, on which the twelfth century seized eagerly as a subject for meditation: "The frequent recollection of the city of Jerusalem and of its king is to us a sweet consolation, a pleasing occasion for meditation and a necessary lightening of our heavy burden."[16] Contemporaries were able to find this theme in some of their favourite authors of the past, for Cassian had expounded it, and Augustine found in the desire for the heavenly Jerusalem the true motive for the Christian life: "If you wish to be armed against temptations in the world, let the desire for the eternal Jerusalem grow and flourish in your hearts."[17]

* See the perceptive remarks of E. Jeauneau, "Nains et Géants", *Entretiens sur la Renaissance du 12e siècle*, pp. 33–4.

In so far as the Jerusalem-devotion of the twelfth century has a single source, it may be found in this and similar passages of Augustine, but the way in which the idea was developed was substantially different from the approach of the early Church. The change may be illustrated by the use made of a passage of Cassian, in which he declared Jerusalem to be "historically speaking the city of the Jews, allegorically the church of Christ, anagogically that celestial city of God which is the mother of us all, tropologically the soul of man."[18] Aelred of Rievaulx perhaps had this passage in mind, and did not depart significantly from it, when he said: "This is the Jerusalem which the Lord Jesus . . . is building out of living stones. . . . It is the holy church, it is each holy congregation, it is each holy soul."[19] In Guibert of Nogent, who unquestionably is echoing Cassian, the symbol has suffered some small but significant changes:

> Jerusalem, historically speaking, is a certain city; allegorically it signifies the holy Church; tropologically (that is, morally) the soul of each of the faithful who strives for the vision of eternal peace; anagogically, it signifies the life of the celestial citizens, who see the face of God revealed in Zion.[20]

The technical meaning of these modes of interpreting the symbol does not concern us here, but the shifts of emphasis are of real interest. The historical sense has moved from "the city of the Jews" (probably with reference to the Old Testament) and is taken to refer to the existing city of Jerusalem; not for nothing was Guibert the author of a Crusading history. The tropological sense is the same, except that Guibert has added a gloss emphasizing that the soul strives for (*anhelat*) the vision of peace, an element found in Augustine and, as we have seen, strongly developed by the twelfth century. The anagogical sense is modified so as to stress that the saints already behold the face of God, an idea not expressed by Cassian and almost certainly not even implied by him. As rewritten by Guibert the definition of Cassian thus enters the age of Crusades, the age of personal longing and the age of individual eschatology, in which the devout soul may hope at death to enter the presence of God.

A still clearer picture emerges from an examination of Jerusalem hymns. For the period before 1050, hymns using the imagery of Jerusalem are rare. The finest of them, *Urbs Beata Jerusalem*, retains the biblical image of the new Jerusalem, coming down out of heaven. Originally it was probably a baptismal hymn, and its theme is the descent of the new Jerusalem, which is embodied in the new members who have become living stones through their baptism:

Blessed City, heavenly Salem,	*Urbs beata Jerusalem*
Vision dear of peace and love,	*dicta pacis visio,*
Who, of living stones upbuilded,	*quae construitur in caelis*
Art the joy of heaven above,	*vivis ex lapidibus,*
And, with angel cohorts circled,	*et angelis co-ornata*
As a bride to earth dost move.	*ut sponsata comite,*
From celestial realms descending,	*Nova veniens e caelo,*
Bridal glory round her shed,	*nuptiali thalamo*
To his presence, decked with jewels,	*praeparata, ut sponsata*
By her Lord shall she be led:	*copuletur domino;*
All her streets, and all her bulwarks,	*plateae et muri ejus*
Of pure gold are fashionèd.	*ex auro purissimo:*
Bright with pearls her portals glitter,	*Portae nitent margaritis*
They are open evermore;	*adytis patentibus,*
And, by virtue of his merits,	*et virtute meritorum*
Thither faithful souls may soar,	*illuc introducitur*
Who for Christ's dear name in this world	*omnis qui pro Christi nomen*
Pain and tribulation bore.*[21]	*hic in mundo premitur.*

The new generation of Jerusalem hymns may be said to begin with Damiani. Instead of the old symbolism (the building up of

---

* For once, the great Victorian hymn-writer J. M. Neale has misconstrued a hymn, but his mistakes reveal so clearly the contrast between the old and new images that I have quoted his version. He has imported into the hymn the assumption that Jerusalem is in heaven, and we go up to it. Since the original thought is of Jerusalem as being prepared in heaven and as descending to earth, the result of Neale's importation of the opposite image is to make his Jerusalem travel disconcertingly up and down. The lines "*art* the joy of heaven *above*" and "thither faithful souls may *soar*" introduce ideas which have no equivalent in the original.

Jerusalem, its descent from heaven), we have a new one: the upward struggle of the soul to the new Jerusalem.

For the fount of life eternal	*Ad perennis vitae fontem*
Thirsts the dry and parchèd mind	*mens sitit nunc arida,*
And the soul its fleshly bondage	*claustra carnis praesto frangi*
Now endeavours to unbind;	*clausa quaerit anima,*
And the exile strives and struggles	*gliscit, ambit, eluctatur*
Fatherland once more to find.[22]	*exsul frui patria.*

It is not surprising, considering his spirit of intense world-renunciation, to find such words on the pen of Peter Damiani; but we realize the strength of the new individualism when we find Hildebert writing in the same style. For all his humanism and love of urbane literature, Hildebert's vision of salvation is of personal escape. His *Hymn to the Trinity* ends in one of the greatest cries of the individual for deliverance:

May I enter Sion's halls,	*Me receptet Syon illa,*
Sight of peace, 'mid David's walls,	*Syon David urbs tranquilla;*
Founded by the Lord of light,	*cuius faber auctor lucis,*
Entered through the Cross's might . . .	*cuius porta lignum crucis . . .*
City, haven of salvation,	*urbs in portu satis tuto,*
Hear my far-off salutation.	*de longinquo te saluto.*
I salute you, and I sigh;	*Te saluto, te suspiro,*
I desire you, and I cry.	*te affecto, te requiro.*
Of your people's exultation	*quantum tui gratulentur,*
And their common jubilation,	*quam festive conviventur,*
Of the love that binds them all,	*quis affectus eos stringat,*
Of the gems that paint the wall	*aut que gemma muros pingat,*
(Finest gems with richest glow)	*quis calcedon, quis iacinctus,*
Only those within can know.	*norunt illi qui sunt intus.*
In that city's golden square,	*in plateis huius urbis,*
Numbered with the perfect there,	*sociatus piis turbis,*
And with Moses and Elijah,	*cum Moyse et Elia*
May I sing my Alleluia.[23]	*pium cantem alleluya.*

It is interesting, and also moving, to observe the same phenomenon here as in Walter of Châtillon. Both poets, although men of the new age, with a greater confidence in the regularity of the created order, have lost the sense of community and also the immediate sense of God's presence. Hildebert can salute the heavenly city only from far off, *de longinquo*. The same is true of Abelard. His tremendous sense of the power of the human intellect never effaced his final loneliness. In the most famous of all Jerusalem hymns, *O quanta qualia*, there is no trace of the old eschatology. Jerusalem no longer comes down from heaven, as in the Scriptures; the coming of the Son of Man to make all things new has no part in Abelard's devotion. Lonely, the exile longs for home:

> Now in the meanwhile, with hearts raised on high,
> We for that country must yearn and must sigh,
> Seeking Jerusalem, dear native land,
> Through our long exile on Babylon's strand.[24]

MYSTICAL THEOLOGY

The conclusion seems justified that, although there was no abandonment of the Church's official eschatology, attention had moved sharply from the salvation of mankind as a whole to the deliverance of the individual. There was a shift away from cosmic expectation to personal piety, or to mystical theology, and the old symbols were exploited in a new sense. As such a hymn as the *Dies irae* shows, the emphasis was increasingly placed on the theme of Judgement, and on the choice which faced the individual believer. This still leaves open one question: Was the new mystical theology itself an individualist one? There are, after all, many mysticisms. It is possible to stress the believer's solidarity with the Church, the redeemed community, as the Bible and most of the Fathers had done. It is possible also to interpret the final union of the soul with God in a way destructive of the person's separate identity—it is even reasonable to do so, for it is hard to see how a creature can remain a distinct unit when brought into the immensity of the Godhead. One element within tradition, especially in the Eastern Church, had accordingly spoken of the "absorption" of the soul into God, and in the writings of pseudo-Dionysius this language had influenced Western thinkers, including William of Saint Thierry.

It may be instructive to consider the element of individualism in the teaching of Saint Bernard, who, because of his strong respect for traditional opinions, was not disposed to take to an extreme the attitudes of his contemporaries. He did, indeed, share many of the distinctively twelfth-century presuppositions. As we saw in Chapter 4, psychology at this time was abandoning a sharp division between love of God and love of self, and was moving towards a more delicate analysis of human "affections". Accordingly, Bernard thought in terms, not of a chasm within the spiritual life, but of development from the fleshly love of self to a pure and spiritual love. A favourite text of both Bernard and William of Saint Thierry was 2 Corinthians 5.16: "though we have known Christ after the flesh, yet now we know him so no more". The intention of Saint Paul here was presumably to contrast his attitudes before and after his conversion, but the autobiographical reference had been missed by later commentators, who usually understood it as opposing the earthly life of Christ to the risen Christ now known by the Church. Bernard and William, by applying it to a man's personal religious experience, gave it a notably new twist, taking it as a comparison between an elementary apprehension of Christ, with which the simple Christian begins, to a deeper spiritual one:

> I think that this was the main cause why the invisible God wished to be seen in the flesh, and as man to converse with men: so as to draw all the affections of fleshly men, who could only love in a fleshly way, to the saving love of his flesh, and thus by stages to lead them to a spiritual love.[25]

This did not imply that spiritual development was easy or unbroken—it is not wholly clear where in this scheme Bernard placed the transition from the secular to the monastic life, which he regarded as a *sine qua non* of full Christian growth. It was, however, a scheme readily accepted in a society where every man was born a Christian, whereas a sharp contrast between the "two loves" was more obviously appropriate to a situation in which the Church was a witnessing minority. This understanding of the nature of growth in the spiritual life brought Bernard close to another popular theme of his age: the importance of intention. "Intention" is not specially a Bernardine word (although he used it on occasions), but the *thing* is crucial in his thought. In a sense the whole drama of the life in Christ consisted, for him, in the purification of motive, or intention, and it was the basis for the classification of the four loves, ascending from loving oneself for the sake of oneself, to loving oneself only for the sake of God. The essential motive power, moreover, which starts a man on this ascent, is compassion for the sufferings of Christ. Bernard is at one with Abelard, and with many of their contemporaries, about the importance of compassion, although for the one it is the starting-point, and for the other almost the whole, of the spiritual life.

While Bernard's presuppositions are thus in tune with the thought of his day, we are still left with the question how far his mysticism is individualistic; or, more precisely, how far his account of man's final goal is phrased in the language of self-fulfilment. This way of speaking was represented in earlier monastic teaching; but, as we have seen, it was modified by other approaches, the language of community and the language of absorption or deification, both of which Bernard used on occasions. If he was a little sparing in using of the Church as a whole the biblical symbols of community, he employed them freely of his monastery. Clairvaux, he taught, *was* Jerusalem. It was a place where men could learn in a common life the love of others and the love of God. It would be absurd to suggest that Bernard was indifferent to the experience of life in community, but we must return to this later to notice a limitation in the significance he was prepared to attach to it.

The language of deification is less characteristic of Saint Bernard, and his use of it was largely confined to his treatise *On the Love of God*, written between 1129 and 1141 and probably influenced by the writings of his friend William of Saint Thierry. It is usual to suggest that Bernard's employment of this language was designed to emphasize a union of wills, and not the absorption of the believer's self into the Godhead. This explanation has the merit of maintaining consistency between the passages concerned and the doctrine of his later works (and, for that matter, of other sections in *On the Love of God*). It is clear, none the less, that in choosing deification language Bernard was putting his emphasis on the unity of the Soul and God, and was relatively little concerned to make a distinction between them:

O holy and chaste love, O sweet and gentle affection, O pure
and undefiled intention of the will—so much the purer and more
undefiled in that nothing of its own is left mingled with it; so
much the sweeter and more gentle, in that what is experienced
is wholly divine! To be thus disposed is to be united with God.
As a little drop of water mixed with a lot of wine seems to
cease to be itself, . . . so it will then be necessary among the
saints for every human affection mysteriously to cease to be
itself, and wholly to be transformed into the will of God.[26]

Sic affici, deificari est; the expression is a strong one, and Bernard
dwells on the necessity for the self to be emptied out: "For in a
sense to lose yourself, as if you were not, and not at all to feel
yourself, but to be emptied of yourself and brought almost to
nothing—that belongs to our conversation in heaven, not to our
human affections."[27] Whatever Bernard meant by the deification
language in *On the Love of God*, he expressed himself differently
in his later works, the sermons on the Song of Songs (1135–53)
and *On Consideration* (*c.* 1150). In these works he spoke of the
individual as fulfilled, not lost, in the encounter with the eternal
Word; and he was prepared to take the language of self-fulfilment
to great lengths.

The sermons on the Song of Songs were designed, from the
beginning, to appeal to private religious experience:

We read today in the book of experience. Turn inwards to
yourselves, and let each of you give heed to his own conscience
about what is to be said. I would discover whether it has been
given to any of you to say, from his own desire, *Let him kiss me
with the kiss of his mouth.*[28]

Self-knowledge is, for Bernard, both the beginning and end of the
spiritual journey: "For you, you are the first; you are also the
last."[29] Accordingly, he insisted that, in the last resort, religious
experience is private and individual, known only to the Bridegroom and the soul:

I do not think that the King has only one couch, but many.
For there is not just one queen, but many; and there are many
concubines, and maidens without number. And each finds her

own secret with the Bridegroom, and says: *My secret is mine, my secret is mine.*[30]

In the later sermons, Bernard was particularly insistent about the continued identity of the soul in its encounter with God. Sermon 71 stressed that the unity, although profound, is one of wills and not of substance, and sermon 83 discussed the bond of love between the soul and the eternal Word. Bernard, looking back over his recent sermons, asked:

> What value has there been in all this work? This, I think: we have learned that every soul—although burdened with sins, ensnared in vices, captured by enticements, captive in exile, imprisoned in the body, stuck in the mire, fast in the mud, transfixed with cares, busy with affairs, oppressed by fear, afflicted with sorrow, troubled by worry, uneasy with suspicion, in short, as the prophet has it, a stranger in the land of enemies, defiled with the dead, counted among those who are in Hades; although, I say, it is so condemned and wretched, yet we have learned that it can perceive within itself not only grounds for the hope of pardon, the hope of mercy, but also grounds on which it may dare to aspire to the marriage of the Word, may without fear enter a bond of society with God, may without alarm take up with the King of angels a sweet yoke of love.[31]

The difficulty about speaking of a "bond of society" or a "yoke of love" between God and the soul is, as Bernard realized, the extreme difference between the two parties. He dealt with this objection in a radical way, by arguing that love essentially creates equality of a sort between lover and beloved: "Love is the only one of all the motions, senses and affections of the soul in which the creature can respond to the Creator, if not perhaps on equal terms, at least in the same terms."[32] Bernard argued that the proper way of conceiving the relationship between the soul and the eternal Word is as a union of two wills, which as entities remain distinct, and even, in the special sense defined, equal:

> That truly is a contract of spiritual and holy matrimony. Indeed, more than a contract: it is a union [*complexus*]. Clearly a union, when to want and reject the same things makes one

spirit of two. Nor should it be feared that the disparity of persons will make the connection of wills limp at all one-sidedly, because love knows no reverence. Love is named from loving, not from honouring. Let him give honour who is full of awe, wonder, fear, amazement. The lover knows nothing of these.[33]

In the spiritual marriage, then, the individual retains his identity. It is the fulfilment, not the annihilation, of the self, and Bernard, in his later works at least, was prepared to speak with remarkable boldness about the continuance of the human will and personality. Whether his earlier excursions into deification language indicated a different view, or merely a different emphasis, the fact remains that they are exceptions within the broad conspectus of Bernard's thought. It is scarcely too much to say that the fulfilment of man is, in the last resort, the fulfilment of the believer's self, which discovers its true identity in a unity of wills with God. The experience of life in community is indispensible in the growth of the Christian, but in the final resort it is a place of preliminary training. The monastery is the school of charity, but the time comes when we must leave school. In this emphasis Bernard was loyal to an important element in Benedictine tradition, in which the Rule was seen as the starting-place of the life of perfection. It would be wrong to press this too far, for there are many fine passages in Bernard's sermons about the communion of saints. Yet it is impossible to avoid the impression that the individual is the true beginning and end of his system of thought. His thinking was much more traditional than that of Abelard, more traditional also than the Jerusalem hymns; but the final verdict must be that Saint Bernard matched their individualist atonement doctrine and eschatology with a mysticism which gave an outstanding place to the individual. That this was his message, he concealed, as we saw, neither from himself nor from his readers: "for you, you are the first; you are also the last".

8 Conclusion

The discovery of the individual was one of the most important cultural developments in the years between 1050 and 1200. It was not confined to any one group of thinkers. Its central features may be found in many different circles: a concern with self-discovery; an interest in the relations between people, and in the role of the individual within society; an assessment of people by their inner intentions rather than by their external acts. These concerns were, moreover, conscious and deliberate. "Know yourself" was one of the most frequently quoted injunctions. The phenomenon which we have been studying was found in some measure in every part of urbane and intelligent society.*

It remains to ask how much this movement contributed to the emergence of the distinctively Western view of the individual. Individualism, as I argued in the first chapter, has taken many forms in the course of our cultural history, and it is not to be expected that all of them will be equally represented in the twelfth century. The most characteristic features of its approach may be summed up in the two expressions "self-discovery" and "humanism". Many examples of both have been quoted. The continuous history of several art-forms and fields of study, which are particularly concerned with the individual, began at this time: autobiography, psychology, the personal portrait, and satire were among them. This interest in self-discovery was intimately related to the conviction that humanity, and human relationships, were

* With the peasantry, the great majority of the population, I have been little concerned in this book. Perhaps the most perceptive contemporary discussion is to be found in Guibert of Nogent, *The Relics of the Saints* (Migne *PL* 156, cols. 607–30). Guibert regards the best popular preaching as a presentation of inner faith, which he associates particularly with confession and confidence in forgiveness. See K. Guth, *Guibert von Nogent und die hochmittelalterl. Kritik an der Reliquienverehrung* (Ottobeuren 1970); and the author's "A Critique of Popular Religion", *Studies in Church History*, vol. 8 (Cambridge 1971), pp. 55–60.

things of real value. In these two crucial ways the heart of the later respect for the individual may be found in the period which we have been studying.

The discovery of the individual was, as we have seen, heavily indebted to the classical and Christian past. The advocates of friendship were consciously concerned to remain within the bounds of a tradition which was rooted in Cicero and had been elaborated, among others, by Cassian and Ambrose. Augustine provided the starting-point for the Cistercian study of psychology, and for some at least of the new attempts at autobiography. Humanists were well versed in the classics, and expounded ethics learned in the school of Cicero and Seneca. Sculptors, by imitating the surviving busts of Roman Emperors, learned to bring a new individuality into their representation of contemporaries. The men of the twelfth century themselves did not attempt to conceal the importance for them of this return to the past, but, when every allowance has been made for it, we must still recognize that the twelfth-century Renaissance was far from being a mere repetition of past ideas and attitudes. Indeed, the charge of simple anti-quarianism, of adopting the style of the past as a matter of "good form", may be made to stick much more firmly on the Renaissance of the fifteenth century than on that of the twelfth. Even when men stayed closest to the classics and the Fathers, we are aware of a sense, not of imitation, but of *rediscovery*. The cult of friendship was regulated by conventions which to us seem artificial, but the reality of the experience is unmistakable. And, because it was a living experience, it acquired a meaning in the twelfth century which it had not had earlier, and played a part in serving the emotional needs, and even the political activities, of monks and scholars, for which no exact analogy can be found in earlier periods. At other times the departure from the past is still more evident. Cistercian psychology progressed a long way beyond that of Augustine. As to the satirists, although they may have known their classical predecessors and revered them, they belong essentially to another world. Their verse forms, marked by the ingenious use of rhythm and rhyme, are unlike those of the past; their subject-matter (above all, the corruptions of the Church) is substantially new; and so is the sense of evil as a cosmic tragedy,

the reality of which can be expressed only through eschatology or
blasphemy. In other areas the break with the past was still more
violent. The years between 1050 and 1200 must be seen, for
example, as a turning-point in the history of Christian devotion.
There developed a new pattern of interior piety, with a growing
sensitivity, marked by personal love for the crucified Lord and
an easy and free-flowing meditation on the life and passion of
Christ; marked also by the regular use of the confessional and the
growing popularity of the position of homage as a posture for
prayer; and by the emergence of the "dying Christ" style of
crucifix. In doctrine the atonement theories of Anselm and Abelard
represented a movement away from the received tradition at a
point of major importance. From all this it will be evident that
the changes which took place in the twelfth century went far
beyond the simple recovery of the classical–Christian past.

The new elements were partly derived from Germanic culture.
The personal character of the lord–man bond, on which the
structure of society so largely depended, encouraged men to
think, in a number of different spheres of activity, in personal
rather than in institutional terms. Its influence may be seen in the
ideal of the "lady" as the object of *fin'amors*, and in the personal
devotion to Christ, which was undoubtedly thought of in lord–
man terms. A more powerful agent still in making for innovation
was the character of the new society, which was unlike the classical
world and also unlike the more primitive Germanic societies which
had preceded it. If there is any one force which may be particular-
ized as creating the new individualism, I have tried to show that
it was the uncertainty created in the minds of men by the opportunities and challenges of a more complex world. The simpler
rules of the immediate past were no longer adequate, and the
more distant culture of the ancients provided inspiration indeed,
but not solutions which could be readily applied to the new
society of Christendom. The situation produced, as such situa-
tions have done in other ages, a new self-consciousness, a capacity
for individual evaluation and criticism, and in general a demand
for individual initiative.

It still remains to summarize our conclusions about the relationship of this discovery of the individual to the later culture of the

West. By some writers it is suggested that there is little connection. Between us and them there is a great gulf fixed, so that it is false to say that in their writings we behold for the first time the lineaments of modern man. The great gulf is the Thomistic revolution of the thirteenth century. It was, according to this view, of the essence of twelfth-century thought that it was theologically orientated. The world had neither meaning nor intelligible pattern until it was related to God. Psychology, as the Cistercians understood it, was the study of the mind or soul *in its ascent to God*, friendship was the relationship of men *in Christ*, and autobiography was the confession of God's goodness and the writer's sin. The revolution of thought in the thirteenth century created, at least in principle, the possibility of a natural and secular outlook, by distinguishing between the realms of nature and supernature, of nature and grace, of reason and revelation. Thanks to the union of Aristotle and Christianity in the works of Aquinas, it was henceforth possible to look at man *either* as a natural being *or* as a being designed for fellowship with God, whereas before the former could not be conceived separately from the latter. From this time onwards, the objective study of the natural order was possible, as was the idea of the secular State.*

There is clearly a great deal of truth in this assessment of the situation, and the emergence of the idea of an autonomous order of nature is of the greatest importance in the development of Europe. Happily for the reader (since the discussion of this question would oblige me to add a second volume to this one), it is not of direct relevance to our theme, and that for three reasons. The first is that, even if the position explained in the preceding paragraph is accepted without qualification, it does not diminish the importance for later history of the twelfth-century discovery of the individual. A sense of the individual's value is not diminished by the fact that he is seen as having a place in a divine purpose. Indeed, in some ways the theological orientation makes

* For important discussions of this controversy see H. Liebeschütz, "Chartres und Bologna, Naturbegriff und Staatsidee bei Johannes von Salisbury", *Archiv für Kulturgeschichte* 50 (1968), p. 3; W. Ullmann, *The Individual and Society in the Middle Ages* (1967); and Gaines Post, *Studies in Medieval Legal Thought* (Princeton 1964), ch. xi.

the individualism the more impressive. When we find that Saint Bernard holds that, in the moment of union with God, a man is not absorbed into the divine being, but remains himself, held by love in a sort of equality with God, we are confronted by an individualism as extreme as any which one can imagine. If this idea is placed beside the view of C. S. Lewis, quoted in the first chapter, that a human being is greater than all nations and civilizations, one realizes the extraordinary continuity of Western Christian thinking. The second reason for not thinking of the twelfth century as divided from us by the chasm of the "Thomist revolution" is that the twelfth-century writers were familiar with the regularity of the natural order. They knew of it (to trace it no further) from Boethius. Walter of Châtillon could regard the order of nature as an accepted fact which provided a tragic contrast with the disorder of man. Indeed, the contrast of the changes of man's moods and the changes of nature's seasons became a commonplace among the troubadours, and the more elaborately learned poets wrote of nature at wearisome length. It is not clear that the thirteenth century was any more "modern" in its concept of nature than the twelfth.* There is, however, another and more decisive reason for being suspicious of any attempt to regard the twelfth century as theologically orientated, and therefore as belonging to an age distinct from our own, and that is the sheer inadequacy of such a description in presenting the wide variety of creative writing at the time. Even the Cistercians (who were

* This sentence should be understood as meaning precisely what it says, for it is not intended to deny that there are differences between twelfth and thirteenth-century concepts of nature. Yet the Aristotelian concept adopted by the thirteenth century was teleological, and saw in nature an ideal order, not simply the totality of what exists; in this sense we can speak of certain practices as "unnatural". This is not at all close to most modern thinkers, who might feel themselves more akin to Walter of Châtillon's sense of a tragic contrast between man and nature. R. W. Southern has recently stressed the continuity between the cosmological ideas of the twelfth century and the thirteenth-century study of the natural order, which was different mainly in being much better informed. See his article, "Medieval Humanism", *Medieval Humanism and other Studies* (Oxford 1970), pp. 29–60, which is a very important contribution to our understanding of the tradition of thought about nature in the twelfth and thirteenth centuries

theologically orientated if anybody was) were characterized by the importance which they attached to man's natural motives or "affections" in his ascent to God. The same is true of friendship. While perfect friendship was for them the union of minds in Christ and with Christ, they were realistic about its character as a natural feature of human society. Aelred was aware that as a young man he had a natural inclination towards friendship, and Bernard insisted that a man must be loved for what he is, not for what one wishes him to be. Indeed, it was the characteristic feature of the most creative minds of the time to discover God, not apart from man, but through man and in man. If one compares their views with the insistence of, for instance, Karl Barth that there is no "point of contact" between God and man, one appreciates how humanist their theology was, and how sensitive to the attitudes and affections of the individual. Abelard is perhaps the extreme example, with his idea that man is saved by "compassion", but I have tried to argue that he was taking further a view essentially similar to that of his contemporaries. Self-knowledge, intention, affection, friendship, humanity—these are the key words of twelfth-century theology. When we move outside the circle of specifically religious thinkers, we find that "theological orientation" is a still more inadequate description. The Archpoet wrote in rebellion against a God-centred view of the world; Chrétien wrote of the relation of the individual to society (at least to society as it imagined itself); and Bernard of Ventadour wrote as if man and a man's loves were all the world. We need not be afraid to look for points of continuity and similarity between that society and our own.

How has the twelfth-century discovery of the individual been conveyed to the modern world? In part the pattern is one of simple continuity. The history of the portrait and of the vernacular lyric has been essentially unbroken since then. The Western attitude to love has been permanently changed by the troubadours and the romances, and their values have even influenced our vocabulary. Men still "court" young ladies, and the age of chivalry is not yet entirely dead. The devotion to the crucified Jesus, movingly expounded by Anselm and the Cistercians, was popularized still more by the Franciscans, and became a permanent part of the life of the Church. The liturgy and the psalter slipped away from the centre of Christian piety, and "to say one's prayers" came to mean praying privately in affective meditation. In claiming a continuity on these points between the twelfth and twentieth centuries, qualifications must be made at each end. Several of these attitudes, or literary forms, probably have an earlier history, which is very ill-recorded, before 1100. We have seen reasons for tracing the dying Christ devotion as far back as late Ottonian Germany, and the vernacular lyric might have been composed, unwritten but not unsung, for a long time before 1100. A more important qualification is that many of these attitudes are more obviously characteristic of Europe before 1914 than of the modern world. Art has turned away from the representational portrait; the lyric, in its conventional form and set pattern of rhyme and metre, has been abandoned by many serious poets, although it continues to be an element in " pop" music; romantic love and chivalry are giving way in face of the demand for sexual equality; and the Church is returning to the liturgy as the essential element in popular devotion. It may be, therefore, that we are asserting a continuity between 1100 and 1900, rather than between 1100 and 1972, and that the dramatic and long chapter in human history entitled "Western civilization" is coming to an end. This is not the main subject of this book, but the point is so important that it is worth noting.

Continuity, however, is not the only relationship between the twelfth century and the Western view of life. More often the pattern is one of loss and recovery. A few things were lost by accident and easily recovered. Abelard's autobiography and his correspondence with Heloïse apparently* remained unknown at her monastery of the Paraclete for a century after her death, but on their discovery they created an interest which has rarely abated, and which has led the two great lovers into places as unexpected as the works of Alexander Pope and the studios of B.B.C. television. There was, however, a loss of the cultural achievement of the twelfth century far more fundamental than the chance

* For this hypothesis, see J. Monfrin, *Abélard, Historia calamitatum* (Paris 1962), introduction, and E. Gilson, *Héloïse et Abélard* (3ᵉ ed., Paris 1964), pp. 208–9.

disappearance* of some of its works. The achievements of the Renaissance of the time were so varied that they contained contradictory tendencies, and its individualism was frustrated by other attitudes. The hierarchical character of the church reform movement was in the long run inimical to the free expression of opinion. The development of civil and canon law was destined to strengthen governmental machinery in both Church and State. The application of logical methods to theology rapidly produced a discipline devoted to the study of revealed propositions, indifferent to biblical history and to the personalities of the biblical writers, and largely divorced from devotion. The existence of contradictory forces can be discerned even in the most creative minds. Bernard of Clairvaux, while deeply committed to self-discovery and to personal experience, readily resorted to authority to silence his opponents. Abelard, the supreme example of the "universal man" of the twelfth-century Renaissance, was a leading champion of the logical techniques which were to dehumanize theology. After 1150 the prospects for a continued development of the individualism and humanism which had achieved so much began to worsen. Peter Lombard's *Sentences*, which were published about 1150, were part of the writing on the wall. They contained much that was enterprising and controversial, and many insights derived from the humanism of the age; but the rigorously logical and propositional structure of the book marked a move away from a close correlation of Christian doctrine with human experience. Meanwhile some of the creative forces were losing their impetus. With the death of William of Saint

* One would not, however, wish to minimize the importance of these disappearances. Some works have gone, and will probably never be discovered, including the letters of Aelred, and the love poems and some theological works of Abelard. Other material, such as the highly influential theological writing of the school of Laon, is only now being identified, and survives in a fragmentary and imperfect way. Some works have survived physically, but have been little read; I would instance the *Commentary on Genesis* by Guibert of Nogent as a book of outstanding interest and originality which has been largely neglected. Finally, some authors have suffered because too much, rather than too little, survived among work ascribed to them: the genuine canon of Anselm's work has only recently been recovered from the huge mass of late medieval devotions which had been attached to his name.

Thierry and of Saint Bernard, the creative period of Cistercian thinking was drawing to a close; their successors were more derivative and, in addition, were increasingly the products of the universities, trained in the predominant theological methods. After notable achievements in our period the love of good letters and the study of the classics also began to fade, stifled by the competition of logic and law. There is, in fact, no sharp break between the twelfth and thirteenth centuries, but it is true to say that, among the various conflicting tendencies which we can observe before 1200, the victory on the whole went to those of law, authority, system, and logic. An eager and critical humanism and the desire for self-exploration are less in evidence after 1200, although examples of both can certainly be found. It was only in the Italian Renaissance that *Latinitas* was once more recovered, along with many of the things which had characterized the twelfth century: the delight in self-expression and self-exploration, the capacity to see the Scriptures, not simply as authorities, but as writings about real men in an actual situation, the original thinking about theological and moral issues.

Our connection with the age of Abelard, then, is partly continuous, partly a question of loss and recovery. It is also perhaps true that we have with it a special sympathy of our own. Then, as now, men faced a crisis of identity. They found themselves in a rapidly changing society, whose stock of knowledge was increasing at a speed which made it difficult to digest. They discovered that inherited ethics and venerated authority did not provide the guidance they needed. Confused over their role in society, they sought new models of behaviour, partly in the distant past; at the same time they spoke with the voice of individual sincerity, convinced that in their personal experience they could find the clues to the meaning of the world. In all this there is much that is common to all men, but I doubt whether these pressures have been felt so strongly by any intervening generation. We feel a natural sympathy for them. Some of them, like Aelred, have almost been discovered by the twentieth century. Up to the last war his works were largely unread, available neither in modern editions nor in translation, but he is now appreciated as one of the most attractive personalities, as well as one of the important thinkers, in an age which abounded in men of individual character and original mind. This has no doubt been made possible by the progress of modern scholarship, but it is also the result of a direct understanding of what Aelred represented. There is something remarkably "modern" about his view that one must renounce one's place in a competitive society in order to discover the basic human values of friendship and self-understanding, and about his belief that God is to be discovered in human relationships. We may or may not accept his solutions, but they speak with a startling immediacy about our own concerns. Aelred and his older contemporaries stood at the beginning of a long history which is just ending, creators of that Western Christendom of whose dissolution we are the witnesses. It is perhaps natural that the same fundamental questions have posed themselves again about our identity as individuals and our function in the world. Although their society and way of life were so different from ours, they speak to us as individuals, with that particular clarity which is the feature of men who know (or at least try to know) themselves.

References

The following abbreviations are employed:
OMLV   Oxford Book of Medieval Latin Verse, ed. F. J. E. Raby, Oxford 1959.
  PL   Patrologia Latina

Where a book has been listed in the *Suggestions for Further Reading*, the reference here will mention only the name of the author and, where necessary, a shortened version of the title.

CHAPTER 1

1. W. H. Auden, *About the House* (London 1966), p. 14.
2. Camara Laye, *The Dark Child* (London 1955), p. 21.
3. *Hamlet*, Act II, Scene 2.
4. C. S. Lewis, *Transposition and other Addresses* (London 1949). p. 33.
5. R. S. Downie and E. Telfer, *Respect for Persons* (London 1969), p. 9.
6. *Julius Caesar*, Act I, Scene 2.
7. Stephen Neill, *A Genuinely Human Existence* (London 1959), p. 16.
8. Marjorie Reeves, *The Influence of Prophecy in the Later Middle Ages* (Oxford 1969), pp. 429–52. See also E. Panofsky, *Renaissance and Renascences in W. Art* (London 1970).
9. David Knowles, "The Humanism of the Twelfth Century", *The Historian and Character* (Cambridge 1963).
10. Bolgar, p. 188.
11. For illustrations of the conventionality of judgement of which the twelfth century was capable, see A. M. Colby, *The Portrait in twelfth-century French Literature* (Geneva 1965).
12. R. Sprandel, *Ivo von Chartres* (Stuttgart 1962), pp. 24–8.
13. Bolgar, p. 26.
14. A. E. Douglas, "Cicero the Philosopher", in *Cicero*, ed. T. A. Dorey (London 1965), pp. 137–8.

15. Cicero, *de Republica* III. xxii. 33.
16. Seneca, *Ep.* 47. I.
17. For the following paragraph, and references, see L. D. Reynolds, *The Medieval Tradition of Seneca's Letters* (Oxford 1965), especially ch. 8–9.
18. On this whole subject see Georg Misch, *A History of Autobiography in Antiquity* (London 1950), especially vol. II.
19. H. R. James, *The Consolation of Philosophy of Boethius* (London 1897), p. 6.
20. Ibid., p. 36.

CHAPTER 2

1. The point is made by M. Seidlmayer, *Currents of Medieval Thought* (Oxford 1960), p. 2 and *passim*.
2. G. Paré, *La renaissance du XIIe siècle* (Paris 1933), p. 144.
3. *OMLV*, no. 128; *English Hymnal* no. 139.
4. *OMLV*, no. 54; *English Hymnal* no. 95.
5. See P. Thoby, *Le crucifixe des origines au Concile de Trente* (Nantes 1959).
6. This idea is fully worked out in an important book by J. Chydenius, *Medieval Institutions and the Old Testament* (Helsinki 1965).
7. See J. M. Wallace-Hadrill, "The *Via Regia* of the Carolingian Age", in B. Smalley, *Trends in Medieval Political Thought* (Oxford 1965), pp. 22–41.
8. Chydenius, op. cit., p. 48.
9. Milo, *Vita Lanfranci* xiii. 33 (Migne, *PL* 150, col. 53 D).
10. *Modus Othinc* in K. Strecker, *Carmina Cantabrigiensia* (M. G. H., Berlin 1926), no. 11.
11. Wipo, "Deeds of Conrad II", in Mommsen and Morrison, *Imperial Lives and Letters of the Eleventh Century* (Columbia 1962), p. 67.
12. *OMLV*, no. 81; *English Hymnal* nos. 621–2.
13. *OMLV*, no. 133; *English Hymnal* no. 130.
14. G. Sitwell, *Odo of Cluny* (London 1958), p. 60.
15. Damiani, *de contemptu saeculi* 30 (Migne, *PL* 145, col. 286 B).
16. *Studia Anselmiana* 18–19 (1947), p. 287.
17. W. von den Steinen, *Der Kosmos des Mittelalters*, p. 372, n. 104.

18. See the discussion by P. Dronke, *The Medieval Lyric* (London 1968), ch. 1.
19. See A. T. Hatto, *The Nibelungenlied* (Penguin Classics 1965), pp. 312–38.
20. Ed. K. Strecker, *Waltharius* (Berlin 1947), lines 248–50.
21. P. Dronke, *Medieval Latin and the . . . Love Lyric* (Oxford 1965) I, p. 39.
22. *OMLV*, no. 122; Waddell, p. 156.

CHAPTER 3

1. Cited by J. Evans, *Life in Medieval France* (London 1957), pp. 14–15.
2. Norbert of Xanten (Migne, *PL* 156, col. 991 C).
3. The formation of the knightly class is discussed by G. Duby, "The Nobility in eleventh and twelfth-century Mâconnais", in F. L. Cheyette, *Lordship and Community in Medieval Europe* (New York 1967), pp. 145–52.
4. *The Alexiad of Anna Comnena*, tr. E. R. A. Sewter (Penguin Books 1969), p. 416.
5. D. C. Douglas, *The Norman Achievement* (London 1969), pp. 124f.
6. Anna Comnena, op. cit., pp. 325–6.
7. G. Duby, "The 'Youth' in twelfth-century aristocratic Society", in F. L. Cheyette, op. cit., pp. 198–209.
8. Migne *PL* 156, col. 684 B.
9. *Cligés*, lines 30–9.
10. *de vita sua*, ed. G. Bourgin (Paris 1907) i. 4, p. 12.
11. Hildebertus, *Carmina Minora*, ed. A. B. Scott (Teubner 1969) no. 36.
12. O. von Simson, *The Gothic Cathedral* (London 1956) pp. 103–7, 120–3.
13. See the discussion by Hans Baron, "Cicero and the Roman civic Spirit", in F. L. Cheyette, op. cit. pp. 296–7.
14. E. Curtis, *European Literature and the Latin Middle Ages* (London 1953) p. 53, n. 54.
15. P. Dronke, *Medieval Latin and the . . . Love Lyric* I, pp. 239–43.
16. Sigebert of Gembloux, *de Scriptoribus Ecclesiasticis* 28 (Migne, *PL* 160, col. 554 B).

17. J. Leclercq, *The Love of Learning and Desire for God*, p. 124.

18. Tr. C. C. Mierow (New York 1928), pp. 323–4.

19. Migne, *PL* 178, col. 1339 A.

20. William of Tyre, *Historia . . . in partibus transmarinis* xix. 3 (Migne, *PL* 201, col. 750 C).

21. *Cur Deus Homo*, praef. (ed. F. S. Schmitt (Edinburgh 1946) II, p. 42).

22. Ibid. I. 7 (Schmitt II, p. 55–6).

23. *Ep.* 190 (Migne, *PL* 182, cols. 1062–3).

CHAPTER 4

1. Migne, *PL* 180, col. 695.

2. Ed. C. C. J. Webb (Oxford 1909) I. p. 19.

3. *Epistola de Incarnatione Verbi* I (Schmitt II, p. 10).

4. F. Wade, "Abelard and Individuality", in *Die Metaphysik im Mittelalter*, ed. Paul Wilpert (Berlin 1963), p. 165, n. 5.

5. *de vita sua* i. 17 (Bourgin, p. 67).

6. *Enarr. in Ps. 130*, 12 (Migne, *PL* 37, col. 1712).

7. *de consideratione* II. iii. 6 (Migne, *PL* 182, cols. 745–6).

8. *Speculum charitatis* I. 5. (Migne, *PL* 195, col. 509 D).

9. *Gesta Dei per Francos*, praef. (Migne, *PL* 156, col. 683 A).

10. *Commentary on Genesis*, prologue (Migne, *PL* 156, cols. 27 B and 28 C).

11. *Serm. 26 in Cant.* (Migne, *PL* 183, col. 909 CD; translation by Eales).

12. *Carmina Burana*, ed. Hilka-Schumann (Heidelberg 1941), no. 70, stanza 12.

13. The passage, which is previously unpublished, is printed with the permission of the Bodleian Library from MS. Laud Misc. 398, fo. 153v–154r.

14. D. Douglas and G. W. Greenaway, *English Historical Documents* II (London 1953), p. 606. The document is discussed by H. E. J. Cowdrey, "Bishop Ermenfrid of Sion and the Penitential Ordinance following the Battle of Hastings", *Journal of Ecclesiastical History* 20 (1969), pp. 225–42.

15. Lines 1136–8 (Oxford version).

16. *Liber visionum* iv (Migne, *PL* 146, col. 354 A).

17. *Analecta Hymnica* 48, p. 221.

18. *Hymni ad usum monasterii Paraclitensis* 1 praef. (Migne *PL* 178, cols. 1773–4; *Analecta Hymnica* 48, p. 144).

19. *Hom.* 13 (Migne, *PL* 158, col. 662 C, where it is wrongly ascribed to Saint Anselm).

20. *Die Sentenzen Rolands*, ed. A. M. Gietl (Freiburg 1891), p. 249.

21. For a wide range of evidence on this point, see A. Teetaert, *La confession aux laïques dans l'Eglise latine* (Paris-Bruges 1926).

22. *Commentary on Genesis*, prologue (Migne, *PL* 156, col. 21 B).

23. *de vita sua*, iii. 19 (Bourgin, p. 221).

24. *de diligendo Deo* x. 28 (Migne, *PL* 182, col. 991 A).

25. D. E. Luscombe, *The School of Peter Abelard* (Cambridge 1969), pp. 175–6.

26. Ed. M. M. Davy, *Deux Traités de l'Amour de Dieu* (Paris 1953), ch. 17. p. 92.

27. Migne, *PL* 180, cols. 717–18.

28. *Liber visionum* xv (Migne, *PL* 146, col. 370 B).

29. *de doctrina spirituali* xi (ibid., col. 270 A).

30. *de tentationibus suis* i (ibid., cols. 32–3).

31. *de vita sua* ii. 3 (Bourgin, p. 113).

32. Ibid., iii. 4 (Bourgin, p. 141).

33. Evans, *Flowering*, pp. 54 and 311.

34. *de vita sua* i. 5 (Bourgin, p. 16).

35. cap. 3 (ed. Monfrin, p. 68).

36. *Römisches Jahrbuch für Kunstgeschichte* 3 (1939), p. 229.

37. P. E. Schramm, *Die deutschen Kaiser und Könige in Bildern ihrer Zeit* (Leipzig 1928), p. 194 and abb. 73.

38. Talbot Rice, *Dark Ages*, pp. 302–3.

39. Evans, *Flowering*, p. 217.

40. E. Bertaux, "Le Tombeau d'une reine de France en Calabre", in *Études d'Histoire et d'Art* (Paris 1911), p. 3.

41. Evans, *Flowering*, p. 310.

42. *La sculpture française au Moyen-Age* (Paris 1946), p. 60.

43. L. Stone, *Sculpture in Britain. The Middle Ages* (Penguin Books 1955), pl. 87.

44. "Zur Frühgeschichte der mittelalterl. Monumentalplastik", in *Westfalen* 35 (1957), p. 37.
45. Josef Déer, "Die Siegel Kaiser Friedrichs I . . .", in *Festschrift Hans R. Hahnloser* (Basle and Sutttgart 1961).

CHAPTER 5

1. *de Spirituali Amicitia* III (ed. J. Dubois, Bruges 1948), pp. 150–2.
2. See R. W. Southern, *Saint Anselm and his Biographer* (Cambridge 1963), pp. 75–6, and Walter Daniel, *Life of Ailred* (ed. F. M. Powicke, p. 40).
3. *de Amicitia* vi. 20.
4. *Catil.* xx. 4.
5. Tr. B. S. James, p. 185.
6. *de Amicitia* ix. 32.
7. James, no. 328, pp. 407–8.
8. Ibid., no. 87.
9. *Odes* I. 3.8. The text of Lawrence of Durham is quoted in Chapter 4 above.
10. Ep. III. 10 (Migne, *PL* 171, col. 289 C).
11. James, no. 389.
12. *Ep.* 85 (ed. Giles Constable, I, p. 222).
13. James, no. 309.
14. *Speculum charitatis* I. 34 (Migne, *PL* 195, col. 543 BC).
15. James, no. 93.
16. *de Spirituali Amicitia* (ed. J. Dubois, pp. 58f).
17. Ibid. (p. 44). Aelred here hesitates to go further than Cassian, who had quoted precisely the same passage in connection with friendship (*Conferences* II. xvi. 13).
18. C. S. Lewis, *The Allegory of Love*, p. 11.
19. P. Dronke, *Medieval Latin and the . . . Love Lyric*, ch. 1.
20. *L'amour et l'occident* (Paris 1939) p. 69.
21. For example, R. R. Bezzola, *Les origines et la formation de la littérature courtoise en occident* (B.E.H.E., Paris 1960) II. ii. pp. 242–315. Contrast the view of A. Jeanroy, *Les Chansons de Guillaume* IX (Paris 1913), p. xvii.
22. P. Dronke, *Medieval Lyric*, ch. 1.

23. J. W. Thompson, *The Literacy of the Laity in the Middle Ages* (New York 1960), pp. 127–30.
24. As cited by Lazar, *Amour courtois et Fin'amors* (Paris 1964), p. 146, n. 40.
25. Ibid., p. 136, and J. Frappier, *Le roman breton* (Paris, "Cours de Sorbonne"), p. 92.
26. Ch. Camproux, *Histoire de la littérature occitane* (Paris 1953), p. 27.
27. P. Bec, *Lyrique occitane*, no. xv.
28. A. Jeanroy, op. cit., IX, 1–6.
29. Ed. C. Appel (Halle 1915) *39*, 1–6.
30. Ibid., *30*, 1–7.
31. Ibid., *31*, 9–10.
32. P. Bec., op. cit., no. xvi.
33. *Sermo ix, in ramis Palmarum* (Migne, *PL* 195, col. 263 D).
34. Ed. C. Appel *21*, 29–32.
35. First letter of Heloïse, ed. J. Monfrin, *Historia Calamitatum* (Paris 1959), p. 114, lines 143f.
36. F. Goldin, *The Mirror of Narcissus in the Courtly Love Lyric* (Cornell 1967), pp. 21–2.
37. *OMLV*, no. 233, lines 73f.

CHAPTER 6

1. See G. B. Ladner, "Homo Viator", *Speculum* (1967).
2. J. A. Yunck, *The Lineage of Lady Meed* (Indiana 1963), especially pp. 13f.
3. See the discussion by A. Morey and C. N. L. Brooke, *Gilbert Foliot and his Letters* (Cambridge 1965), pp. 166–87.
4. J. A. Yunck, op. cit., pp. 47f.
5. *OMLV*, no. 160; *English Hymnal* no. 495.
6. *de consideratione* I. iv. 5.
7. T. Wright, *Latin Poems attributed to Walter Mapes* (Camden Soc. 1841), p. 41.
8. *OMLV*, no. 196.
9. K. Strecker, *Moralisch-Satirische Gedichte Walters von Chatillon* (Heidelberg 1929), no. 16.
10. Book I, Song 5.

11. *OMLV*, no. 200.
12. J. A. Yunck, op. cit., pp. 76–8.
13. Ibid., pp. 70–6.
14. T. Wright, op. cit., p. 5. Other MSS. read *in Neustria*, so the English origin of the poem cannot be taken for granted.
15. T. Wright, op. cit., p. 7.
16. Ibid., p. 20.
17. See F. J. E. Raby, *Secular Latin Poetry in the Middle Ages* (Oxford 1934), II. pp. 339–41, for a succinct discussion of the obscure origin of Golias and the Goliards.
18. *Wandering Scholars* (Penguin Books 1954), p. 175.
19. *OMLV*, no. 183; Waddell, p. 182.
20. Waddell, p. 206.
21. *Erec et Enide*, lines 2459–62 (tr. W. W. Comfort, p. 32).
22. Ibid., line 6479 (p. 84).
23. Ibid., lines 5636–8 (p. 73).
24. *The Knight of the Lion*, lines 5176–7 (p. 247).
25. Ibid., lines 1982 and 2015f (p. 206).
26. For example, D. W. Robertson, "The doctrine of charity in medieval literary gardens", *Speculum* 26 (1951), p. 24; B. N. Sargent, "L' autre chez Chrétien de Troyes", *Cahiers de civilisation médiévale* 10 (1967), p. 199; and J. Mandel, "Elements in the 'Charette' world", *Modern Philology* 62 (1964–5), p. 97.
27. *The Story of the Grail*, lines 558–62.

CHAPTER 7

1. *OMLV*, no. 133; *English Hymnal*, no. 130.
2. For examples, see Migne, *PL* 40, col. 1096, and 112, col. 1427 C.
3. Migne, *PL* 106, col. 57.
4. Aelred, *La Vie de Recluse* (ed. C. Dumont (Paris 1961)).
5. Cap. xv (col. 88 C).
6. Cap. xviii (cols. 96–7).
7. Dumont, op. cit., p. 104.
8. Ibid., p. 134.
9. Walter Daniel, *Vita*, p. 61.
10. *OMLV*, no. 171; Waddell, pp. 178–9.

11. Migne, *PL* 178, col. 836 AB.
12. Ed. A. Landgraf, *Commentarius in Epistolas Pauli* (Indiana 1939), II, p. 292.
13. H. de Lubac, *Corpus Mysticum* (Paris 1949), p. 322.
14. Ibid., p. 320.
15. Migne, *PL* 145, col. 748 C.
16. *Mélanges J. Lebreton* (Recherches des sciences religieuses 1952), p. 330.
17. *Enarr. in Ps.* 136, 22.
18. *Collations* 14, 8.
19. Migne, *PL* 195, col. 228 D.
20. Guibert, *Commentary on Genesis*, prologue (Migne, *PL* 156, col. 26 A).
21. *OMLV*, no. 63; *English Hymnal* no. 169.
22. *OMLV*, no. 135.
23. *OMLV*, no. 159; Hildebertus, *Carmina Minora* (ed. A. B. Scott (Teubner 1969)), no. 55.
24. *OMLV*, no. 169; *English Hymnal*, no. 465; Waddell, p. 174.
25. *Sermo 20 in Cant.* v. 6 (Migne, *PL* 183, col. 870 B).
26. *de diligendo Deo* x. 28. (Migne, *PL* 182, col. 991 AB).
27. Ibid. x. 27 (ibid., col. 990 C).
28. *Sermo 3 in Cant.* i. 1. (Migne, *PL* 183, col. 794 A).
29. *de consideratione* II. iii. 6 (Migne *PL* 182, col. 746 A).
30. *Sermo 23 in Cant.* iv. 9, citing Isa. 24.16 (Vulgate).
31. *Sermo 83 in Cant.* i. 1 (Migne, *PL* 183, col. 1181 CD).
32. Ibid., ii. 4 (ibid., col. 1183 BC).
33. Ibid., i. 3 (ibid., col. 1182 CD). On this question, see the discussion in Gilson, *Mystical Theology*.

Suggestions for Further Reading

Full bibliographies may be found in several of the works listed below, and detailed references are provided in the separate table. The object of these suggestions is to mention those books which are most directly related to the theme of the book, and to indicate some translations of medieval authors who have been discussed.

MODERN WORKS

M. Bloch, *Feudal Society*. London 1962.

R. R. Bolgar, *The Classical Heritage and its Beneficiaries*. Cambridge 1954.

— (ed.), *Classical Influences on European Culture, 500–1500*. Cambridge 1971.

C. N. L. Brooke, *The Twelfth Century Renaissance*. London 1969.

H. Davenson, *Les troubadours*. Paris 1961.

P. Dronke, *Medieval Latin and the Rise of the European Love Lyric*. Oxford 1965.

— *The Medieval Lyric*. London 1968.

— *Poetic Individuality in the Middle Ages*. Oxford 1970.

J. Evans, (ed.), *The Flowering of the Middle Ages*. London 1966.

J. Frappier, *Chrétien de Troyes*. Paris 1957.

M. de Gandillac and E. Jeauneau, *Entretiens sur la Renaissance du 12ᵉ siècle*. Paris 1968.

E. H. Gilson, *Héloise et Abélard*. Paris 1964.

— *The Mystical Theology of Saint Bernard*. London 1940.

L. Grane, *Peter Abelard*. London 1970.

V. H. H. Green, *Medieval Civilization in Western Europe*. London 1971.

C. H. Haskins, *The Renaissance of the Twelfth Century*. Cambridge, Mass. 1927.

D. Knowles, "The Humanism of the Twelfth Century", *The Historian and Character*. Cambridge 1963.

G. B. Ladner, "Homo Viator: Medieval Ideas on Alienation and Order", *Speculum* 42, 1967, pp. 233–259.

M. Lazar, *Amour courtois et Fin'amors*. Paris 1964.

J. Leclercq, *The Love of Learning and the Desire for God*. New York 1961.

J. Le Goff, *La civilisation de l'occident mediéval*. Paris 1964.

C. S. Lewis, *The Allegory of Love*. Oxford 1936.

H. Liebeschuetz, *Medieval Humanism in the Life and Writings of John of Salisbury*. London 1950.

P. von Moos, *Hildebert von Lavardin 1056–1133*. Stuttgart 1965.

F. J. E. Raby, *A History of Christian Latin Poetry*. 2nd edn, Oxford 1953.

— *A History of Secular Latin Poetry in the Middle Ages*. 2nd edn, Oxford 1957.

H. Schauwecker, *Otloh von St Emmeram. Ein Beitrag zur Bildungs— und Frömmigkeitsgeschichte des II Jhdts*. Munich 1965.

M. Seidlmayer, *Currents of Medieval Thought*. Oxford 1960.

R. W. Southern, *The Making of the Middle Ages*. London 1953.

— *Saint Anselm and His Biographer*. Cambridge 1963.

— *Medieval Humanism and other Studies*. Oxford 1970.

R. Sprandel, *Ivo von Chartres*. Stuttgart 1962.

A. Squire, *Aelred of Rievaulx*. London 1969.

D. Talbot Rice, ed., *The Dark Ages*. London 1965.

W. von den Steinen, *Der Kosmos des Mittelalters. Von Karl dem Grossen zu Bernhard von Clairvaux*. Berne–Munich 1959.

W. Ullmann, *The Individual and Society in the Middle Ages*. Baltimore 1966, London 1967.

E. Vinaver, *The Rise of Romance*. Oxford 1971.

TRANSLATIONS: SELECTIONS

P. Bec, *Petite Anthologie de la lyrique occitane du Moyen Age*. Paris, 1965.

E. R. Fairweather, *A Scholastic Miscellany: Anselm to Occam*. London 1956.

D. Herlihy, *Medieval Culture and Society*. Harper Torchbooks 1968.

H. Waddell, *Medieval Latin Lyrics*. Penguin Books 1952.

TRANSLATIONS: PARTICULAR AUTHORS

PETER ABELARD

D. E. Luscombe, *Peter Abelard's Ethics*. Oxford 1971.

C. K. Scott Moncrieff, *The Letters of Abelard and Héloïse*. London 1925.

J. R. McCallum, *Abailard's Ethics*. Oxford 1935.

AELRED OF RIEVAULX

G. Webb and A. Walker, *The Mirror of Charity*. London 1962.

F. M. Powicke, ed., *The Life of Ailred of Rievaulx by Walter Daniel.* London 1950.

BERNARD OF CLAIRVAUX
B. S. James, *The Letters of Saint Bernard of Clairvaux.* London 1953.
The Works of Bernard of Clairvaux. Cistercian Fathers Series. Shannon 1970–

BERNARD OF VENTADOUR
S. G. Nichols and J. A. Galm, *The Songs of Bernart de Ventadorn.* Chapel Hill 1962.

CHRÉTIEN DE TROYES
W. W. Comfort, *Chrétien de Troyes, Arthurian Romances.* Everyman 1914, repr. 1968.
R. W. Linker, *The Story of the Grail.* Chapel Hill 1952.

PETER DAMIANI
P. McNulty, *Selected Writings on the Spiritual Life.* London 1959.

GUIBERT OF NOGENT
C. C. S. Bland, *The Autobiography of Guibert abbot of Nogent.* London 1925.
John F. Benton, *Self and Society in Medieval France. The Memoirs of Abbot Guibert of Nogent.* Harper Torchbooks 1970.

NIBELUNGENLIED
A. T. Hatto, *The Nibelungenlied.* Penguin Books 1965.

ODO OF CLUNY
G. Sitwell, *Saint Odo of Cluny.* London 1958.

SONG OF ROLAND
D. Sayers, *The Song of Roland.* Penguin Books 1957.

RUODLIEB
E. H. Zeydel, *Ruodlieb.* New York 1969.

WILLIAM OF SAINT THIERRY
G. Webb and A. Walker, *On the Nature and Dignity of Love.* London 1956.

Index

Medieval scholars are indexed under their Christian names. References to particular books will be found under the name of their authors.

Aachen 89
Abelard *see* Peter
Acts of the Apostles 102
Adela, countess of Blois 43–5
Adso, abb. of Montier 145
Aelred, abb. of Rievaulx xvi–xviii, 8–9, 29, 47, 49, 54, 66, 76, 79, 96, 98, 100–1, 105–6, 116, 141–2, 149, 163, 165n–7
affectus, affection 8, 15, 75–9, 105, 151, 153, 155–6, 163
Agnes, empress 73
Alan of Lille 15
Albinus, martyr 128
Alexander III, pope xvii, 62, 73, 125
Alexandria 16, 38–9
Alexius I Comnenus 43
alienation 122, 133, 137
Amaury I, k. of Jerusalem 61
Ambrose, St 16, 18, 55, 98, 159
amicitia see friendship
amor de lonh 113–14, 118
Anacletus II, pope 145
anima, mind, soul xvii, 64–6, 69, 76–8, 102–3, 107, 132, 147, 149, 151, 156
Anno, scribe 89
Anselm, abp. of Canterbury xv–xvi, 8, 29, 49, 51, 59, 61, 63–4, 76, 82–3, 96–7, 99, 101, 124, 143, 160, 163, 165n
Anselm of Laon xvi, 83–4, 86
Antichrist 54, 127, 145, 148
Antioch 16, 39, 42
Apocalypse of Golias 129–30
Archpoet xvii, 70, 121, 130–2, 163
aristocracy, nobility 26–7, 31–4, 38n, 40–5, 49, 53, 107, 110, 113, 117, 121, 133; *see also* courts
Aristotle 2, 17, 53, 74, 98, 161–2n

Arthur, king 133
atonement 59–64, 142–4, 148, 157, 160
Atto, bp. of Trier 104
Aubert, M. 91
Auden, W. H. 1–2
Augustine, St 16–18, 52, 55, 58, 66, 76–80, 84, 144, 148–9, 159
Augustus, emp. 117
Aulén, G. 59n
autobiography 4, 16–17, 32, 50, 69–70, 79–86, 97–8, 113–14, 131, 153, 158–9, 161, 164
Autun 90

Barbarossa *see* Frederick
Barth, K. 163
Batany, J. 30n
Baudri, abb. of Bourgueil 45, 97, 111
Beauvais 83
Benedict, Rule of 52–3, 58, 157
Benton, J. F. 83n
Bernard of Chartres 55
Bernard, abb. of Clairvaux xvi–xvii, 13, 47–9, 54, 62–3, 66–7, 74–5, 97–100, 102–6, 118–19, 123–4, 139, 142, 145, 152–7, 162–3, 165–6
Bernard of Cluny xvii, 123–4
Bernard of Ventadour xvii, 45, 96, 111, 113–18, 134, 163
Bertrand de Born 45, 117
Bible: 11, 16, 37, 52, 57, 61, 67, 70, 82–3, 101, 106, 132, 139, 150, 152, 165–6; Old Testament 24–5, 68, 98, 149; New Testament 5, 11–12, 18, 30, 98; *see also particular books*
biography 4, 8, 32, 79, 98, 100
Boethius 17–18, 53, 55, 127, 162
Bohemond, p. of Antioch 42
Bolgar, R. R. 6–7, 13

Bologna 125, 161n
Bourges 48
Bridbury, A. R. 38n
Bruges 39–40
Bultot, R. 30n

Candidus Bruno 141
canon law 12–13, 52, 58–60, 107, 124–6, 165
Cappenberg xvii, 93–5; pl. 3
carnal *see* flesh
Carolingian 21, 25, 35, 88n, 98, 140–2
Carthusian 83
Cassian 16, 18, 98, 106, 148–9, 159
chansons de geste see epics
Charlemagne 8, 21, 25–6, 92, 94
Chartres xv, 48, 161n
Chaucer 122
chivalry: knightly class 26, 33n, 37, 41, 43–4, 47, 50, 54, 92–4, 108, 121–2, 133–8, 163–4
Chrétien de Troyes xviii, 9, 37, 45, 50, 56, 75–6, 111, 121–2, 133–8, 163
Christ *see* Jesus
Church: concept of 11–13, 24–5, 59, 70, 139, 144, 147, 149, 152–3; buildings of xvii, 27–8, 39, 48, 52, 71, 79, 90
Cicero 14–16, 18, 47, 53–5, 69, 98, 100–2, 159
Cimabue 5
Cistercians xv, 12–13, 48–9, 53–4, 58, 66, 76–9, 83, 99–101, 106, 117–19, 147, 159, 161–3, 166; *see also* Aelred; Bernard; William
Cîteaux *see* Cistercians
city, cultural influence of 13–16, 20, 37–40, 49–50, 53
Clairvaux *see* Bernard
classics, influence of 7–10, 13–21, 47–8, 50–7, 61, 68, 78–9, 81, 83, 93–5, 98–9, 108, 111, 123–4, 127, 132, 159–60, 166; *see also particular writers*
Cluny 22, 27, 30, 32, 71, 74
Cologne *see* Gero, Nicholas of Verdun
confession xvii, 70–5, 84, 131–2, 158n, 160–1

Conrad II, emp. 25
Constantine emp. 88
Cosenza 89
Courcelle, P. 17n
courtly love 35–6, 44–5, 108–20, 160
courts, as cultural centres 21–2, 30, 33, 43, 45–7, 49, 97, 100, 104, 110–12, 130, 134–5, 138
crucifix . 23, 29, 140–2, 160; pl. 5, 6, 7, 8
Crusades xv, xviii, 42–3, 49, 66, 83, 89, 122, 142, 146, 149

Damian *see* Peter Damiani
David, k. of Israel 25, 68–9, 98, 151
David I, k. of Scotland 100
Delphi 56, 64–5, 78
de Rougemont, D. 109
devil, rights of 61–2, 143
Dies irae 152
doubt 61, 82
Douglas, A. E. 14
drama, liturgical 29–30
Dronke, P. 68n
Duby, G. 38n
Dulcis Jesu memoria 119
Durand, abb. of Moissac 90–1
Durham 100; *see also* Lawrence

Eadwine of Canterbury xvii, 85
Ebles of Ventadour 109
Einhard 8
Eleanor, duchess of Aquitaine xvi–xvii, 44, 91, 111, 133; pl. 4
epics 33–5, 44, 48, 113; *see also particular poems*
Erasmus 5, 8
eremitical movement 16, 22, 30–2, 39–40, 66, 71, 74
eschatology 124, 127–30, 139, 144–52, 157, 160
ethic, ethics 3–4, 11, 14, 32, 43, 46–7, 53, 55, 64, 73–5, 121–2, 134–5, 137, 159, 166
Eucharist 12, 59, 142
Eugenius III, pope 66
Eve 90
Everwin, apprentice 90

Fathers, influence of 2, 5, 16, 20–1, 24–5, 37, 39, 52–3, 55, 57–63, 74, 82–3, 98–9, 108, 139–40, 146, 149,

Fathers, influence of—*cont.*
  152, 159–60; *see also particular authors*
fin'amors see courtly love
flesh, concept of 67, 77, 105, 151, 153
florilegia 54–5
Fontevrault xviii, 91; pl. 4
Forsyth, I. H. 29n
Franciscans 142, 146, 163
Frederick I "Barbarossa", emp. xvii, 54, 93–5, 131; pl. 3
French, literature 9, 33, 48, 109
friendship 14–16, 18, 34, 54–5, 68–9, 79, 96–108, 117–18, 142, 159, 161, 163
Fulbert, bp. of Chartres 22, 50–1
Fulda 80

Gaudri, bp. of Laon 85
Genesis 83, 85, 165n
Genicot, L. 26
Geoffrey, c. of Anjou xvii, 91; pl. 2
Gerald of Wales 47
Gerard of Aurillac 26
Gerard of Clairvaux 67, 98
German, literature 33, 109
Gero, abp. of Cologne 89, 140; pl. 6
Gibbon, E. 24
Gilbert de la Porrée 52
Gilbert Foliot 97, 123
Gilson, E. 119
Giotto 5
Gislebert of Autun 90
"Glanvil" 46
Godfrey de Huy 93
Godfrey of St Victor 15
Goliards 130–1
Gospel of Silver Mark 128
Gothic 39, 48, 52, 90
grammar 50, 55, 135n
Gratian 126
Gregory VII, pope xv, 62
Grundmann, H. 93n
Guibert, abb. of Nogent xv–xvi, 8, 49–50, 65–7, 74, 83–6, 111, 149, 158n
Guth, K. 158n
Guy de Bazoches 39

Haimeric, cardinal 104

Hastings, b. of 70, 74
Heloise 84, 97, 111, 116–17, 142, 164
Henry II, emp. 89
Henry III, emp. xv
Henry IV, emp. xv, 92
Henry VI, emp. 94
Henry I, k. of England xvi, 44–5, 56, 100, 107n
Henry II, k. of England, c. of Anjou xvii–xviii, 44, 46–7, 91, 107n, 125–6; pl. 4
Henry, son of H. II, k. of England 44
Henry III, k. of England 89
hermits *see* eremitical
Hexham 49, 100
Hilary, St 52
Hildebert of Lavardin xv–xvi, 47, 51–2, 56, 97, 99, 102–4, 124, 148, 151
Hildebert of Prague 90
history 11, 14, 17, 54, 66, 74, 83, 144, 149
Hobbes, T. 3
Hoffman, K. 90n, 93n
Hohenstaufen 92–5
Horace 69, 103, 123, 132
Hugh of Prémontré 102
humanism, humanists 3, 5–11, 14–15, 17, 33n, 45–55, 63, 69, 97, 99–100, 104, 124–7, 151, 158–9, 163, 165–6
Humbert, cardinal 80
hymns 22–3, 27–8, 33, 71–2, 84, 119, 131, 142–3, 149–52, 157

Iam dulcis amica 35–6
Innocent II, pope 104
Innocent III, pope 62
intention 60, 66, 73–5, 153–5, 158, 163
In trutina mentis dubia 68–9
Isabel, q. of France 89
Ivo, bp. of Chartres xv, 10, 124–5
Ivo, friend of Aelred 100, 106

James, St 74
Jaufre Rudel xvii, 96, 113–14
Jeauneau, E. 57n, 148n
Jerome, St 81, 98
Jerusalem xv, xviii, 22, 61, 83, 119, 148–52, 154, 157

Jesus Christ: 11–12, 15–16, 23–5, 27, 30, 61, 64, 87, 89, 98, 106, 118–20, 124, 128, 132–3, 149–50, 153, 160–1, 163–4; passion and crucifixion 22–3, 27, 29, 36, 56, 59, 75, 116, 139–44, 146, 151, 154; resurrection; Easter 22, 27–9, 36, 143–5; Epiphany 29
John, St, evangelist 23, 106, 140
John, St, the divine 129
John, St, of Damascus 78
John, k. of England 91, 107n
John, abb. of Fécamp xv, 22
John of Salerno 79
John of Salisbury xvii–xviii, 8, 47, 49, 53–5, 63–4, 104, 125, 161n
joie 45, 114–17
Jonathan, friend of David 68–9, 98
Jongkees, A. G. 50n
Juvenal 123, 132

Kant, E. 3
Keller, H. 88
king, authority of 24–7, 36, 40, 47–8, 87–95
Knights *see* chivalry
Knowles, D. 6, 17n
Know yourself see self-knowledge

lady, ideal of 34–5, 44–5, 54, 75, 90, 96–7, 108, 112–19, 133–7, 160
Langres 85
Languedoc *see* Provençal
Laon 75, 84, 165; *see also* Anselm; Gaudri
Lateran, 4th C. of 73
Latin: language 17, 28, 33, 74, 132; literature in M.A. 5, 7–9, 35, 50–1, 68–9, 97, 110–11, 122–4, 131, 166
law, lawyers 15, 46–9, 52–3, 124–6, 165–6; *see also* canon law
Lawrence of Durham xvi, 68–9, 100, 103
Lech, b. of 21
Leclercq, J. 57
Le Mans 91; pl. 2
letters (correspondence) 15, 79, 84, 96–9, 102–6, 111, 165n
Lewis, C. S. 3, 108–9, 162
Liebeschütz, H. 161n

Liége 66
Limoges 110
liturgical drama 29–30
liturgy 9, 11, 21–30, 36, 58, 93, 164
Locke, J. 3
Lothar of Supplinburg, emp. 41
Louis VI, k. of France xvi
Louis VII, k. of France xvi
Louis IX, k. of France 89
Louis, son of Louis IX 89
Lubac, H. de 146
Lucan 55, 81
Luscombe, D. E. 75n
Luther, M. 5, 73
lyric verse 4, 8, 14, 33, 35–6, 68–70, 163–4; *see also* Latin; troubadours

Manichees 14
Marbod, bp. of Rennes 45, 51, 111, 124
Marcabru xvi, 44–5, 112–13
Marie, countess of Champagne 133
marriage 34–5, 41, 45, 58, 62, 98, 107–8, 117, 134–5, 147, 156–7
Mary, mother of Christ 23, 29, 114, 119, 140
Mary Magdalene 28, 71–2
Mass *see* Eucharist
Matilda, q. of England 44
meditation 8, 140–1, 146–8, 160
Merseburg 91; pl. 1
Michaelangelo 5
millenarianism 145–6
mirror xvii, 100, 116, 118–20
Moissac 90

nature (naturalism) 1, 11, 18, 51–2, 79, 82, 90–3, 114–15, 126–7, 144, 151, 161–2
Neale, J. M. 150n
Neill, bp. Stephen 5
Neoplatonism 14, 17–18
Newman, F. X. 110n
New Testament *see* Bible
Nibelungenlied 33n, 34
Nicholas of Verdun xviii, 140; pl. 8
Nicholas, messenger 105
nobility *see* aristocracy
Norbert of Xanten 83, 104

Odo, abb. of Cluny 26, 30, 32, 79, 127, 145

Offa, k. of Mercia 88n, 89n
officiales 46, 125
Old Testament *see* Bible
order *see* nature
Otloh of St Emmeram xv, 32, 65, 71, 79–83
Otto I, emp. 21–2
Otto III, emp. 21–2, 25, 87, 89
Otto, c. of Cappenberg 93
Otto, bp. of Freising xvii, 50n, 59, 148
Ottonian 21–2, 25, 90, 164
Ovid 9, 35, 55–7, 97, 108–9, 111, 132–3

papacy 13, 46, 58, 62–3, 80, 92, 104, 124–6, 128–9
Paraclete, convent of xvi, 84, 142, 164
paradise 101, 106
Paris xvi, 13, 38–9, 48–50n
Paschal II, pope 84
Paul, St 11, 16, 24, 153
penance, penitence 24, 70–2, 84
Peter Abelard xvi–xvii, 47, 49, 52–4, 59–60, 62–5, 68, 70–5, 82–6, 97, 111, 116, 142–5, 148, 152, 154, 157, 160, 163–6
Peter of Blois 8, 46, 97, 100
Peter Damiani xv, 22, 31–2, 66, 73, 123, 147, 150–1
Peter Lombard xvii, 49, 63, 146, 165
Peter the Venerable 97, 99, 102, 104–5
Philip III, k. of France 89
Philip, c. of Flanders 133
pilgrimage 29, 38–9, 73, 122
Plato 65, 98; *see also* Neoplatonism
Pope, Alexander 164
portrait xvii, 4, 65, 70, 85–95, 136, 158, 163–4
Post, G. 161n
prayer 22, 72, 102–3, 142, 164–5n; *see also* liturgy; meditation
preaching 40, 45, 67, 73–4, 98, 106–7, 122, 145–6, 155–7, 158n
Premonstratensians 83; *see also* Hugh, Norbert
Provençal 33, 48; *see also* troubadours

psychology 1, 3, 70, 76–9, 83, 109, 112, 135–6, 153, 158–9, 161

quest 44, 119, 136–7

Rahewin 94
Rainald of Dassel, abp. of Cologne 130
Ratherius of Verona 79
Raoul of Cambrai 34
relics 29, 38, 83, 93–4, 128, 158n
Renaissance: concept 5–7, 21; Carolingian 21, 35, 98; twelfth century 6–7, 9, 21, 30; ch. 3; 127, 159, 165; fifteenth century 5–7, 21, 48, 159, 166
resurrection (of saints) 22, 144–5, 147; *see also* Jesus Christ
Rheims 66
Richard I, k. of England 107n
Rievaulx *see* Aelred
Robert of Rhuddlan 42
Robertson, D. W. 110n
Roland, Song of xv, 26, 33n, 34, 71
Rome, city of 51–2, 73, 93, 103; *see also* classics; papacy
Romuald, St 22, 31–2
Rougemont, Denis de 100
Rousseau, J. J. 3
Rudolf of Suabia, anti-king xv, 91–3; pl. 1
Rufinus, martyr 128
Ruodlieb xv, 134n

Saint-Denis xvii, 38, 48, 52, 79; *see also* Suger
Saint-Germer-de-Fly 83
saints 11, 29, 49, 52, 60, 62, 83, 144–7, 149, 155, 157, 158n
Sallust 14, 102
Samson 68n
Sant' Angelo in Formis 32
satire 8, 45, 47, 54, 75, 85–6, 108, 110, 112–13, 117, 122–33, 135, 138, 158–9
schools 5, 9, 38–9, 46, 48, 50–1, 62, 75, 78, 80–1, 85–6, 97, 133, 135n, 165–6
Schrade, H. 92
Scriptures *see* Bible
secular society *see* world

self-knowledge   4, 7–8, 10, 15–16, 18,
    31–2, 36–7, 54, 56; ch. 4; 99, 118–
    19, 137–8, 155–8, 160, 163, 166
Seneca   14–16, 18, 53, 56, 98, 159
Sens   xvii, 48
Serlo of Wilton   55–6
Shakespeare, W.   3–4, 54, 136
Simon, friend of Aelred   105
Song of Roland   xv, 26, 33n, 34, 71
Song of Songs   xvi, 35, 56, 64–5, 78,
    105–7, 155–7
soul   *see anima*
Southern, R. W.   6n, 162n
Stephen, k. of England   125
Suetonius   8, 14
Suger, abb. of Saint-Denis   xvii, 52,
    79, 99n

Tegernsee   80–1
Terence   9
Theobald, abp. of Canterbury   104
Thomas Becket, abp. of Canterbury
    xviii, 46–7, 123, 125–6
Thomism   161–2
Topsfield, D. W.   110n
translatio studii   36, 50, 148
troubadours   9, 33, 43–5, 48, 96,
    107–20, 162–3; *see also particular
    writers*
Troy   54

Ullmann, Walter   6, 161n
universities   *see* schools
Urbs beata Jerusalem   150

Venantius Fortunatus   22–3
Ventadour   111; *see also* Bernard;
    Ebles
verai' amors   see courtly love
vernacular   8–9, 33, 35, 48–9, 68, 97,
    109–11, 127, 163–4; *see also* French;
    Provençal
Victor II, pope   80
Virgil   55–7, 111

Waddell, H.   131
Walter of Châtillon   xviii,   126–8,
    131–3, 145, 148, 151, 162
Walter Daniel   100–1, 142
Waltharius   33n, 34–5
Waverley   49
Westminster   89
White Ship   56
William I, k. of England   25, 70, 83,
    107n
William II, k. of England   29
William, son of Henry I   56
William Marshal, e. of Pembroke
    41, 44
William IX, c. of Poitou, d. of
    Aquitaine   xv–xvi, 43, 109–12
William of St Thierry   xvi–xvii, 49,
    64–6, 75–9, 147, 152–4, 165–6
William, abp. of Tyre   61
Wipo   27–8
Worcester   91
world, concept of   16, 21, 30–1, 53–4,
    80–1, 99, 121, 123–4, 127, 151, 161

youth   43–5